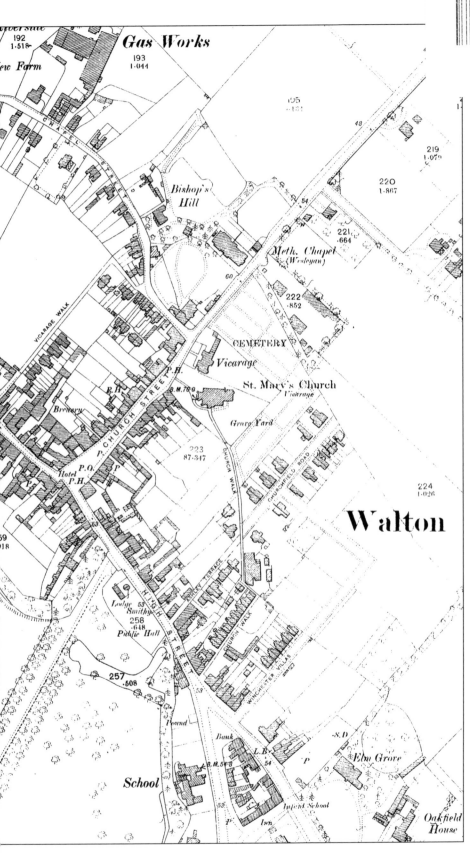

# WALTON
# PAST

A family group outside the *Bear* in Bridge Street in the 1890s.

# WALTON PAST

Bryan Ellis

Phillimore

2002

Published by
PHILLIMORE & CO. LTD
Shopwyke Manor Barn, Chichester, West Sussex

ISBN 1 86077 211 0

Printed and bound in Great Britain by
BIDDLES LTD
Guildford, Surrey

# Contents

# List of Illustrations

*Frontispiece*: The *Bear* in Bridge Street in the 1890s

# Acknowledgements

The Walton and Weybridge Local History Society was founded in 1964. Since then it has produced a quarterly newsletter, *Dial Stone*, and a steady stream of booklets and monographs on the history of our area. These studies have been the principal source of information for this book. I should like to pay tribute to the society's writers and researchers—notably Michael Blackman, who wrote *A Short History of Walton-on-Thames*, and the late John Stonebanks, Jim Forge and George Greenwood, and to thank Joyce Greenwood for allowing me to draw on her husband's unpublished Notes on the History of Walton. I am also greatly indebted to the society's present and recent officers and committee for their encouragement and support—in particular John Pulford senior, who read my manuscript and offered wise comments and essential corrections, and John Pulford junior, who not only did this but drew the map which forms the book's back endpaper.

Another local institution from which I have received tremendous help is the Elmbridge Museum in Weybridge, whose unrivalled photographic collection provided more than a hundred of the illustrations I have used. I should like to record my gratitude to Michael Rowe, the museum manager, Melanie Parker his deputy, Viv McKenzie and Sue Slight, and also to Jocelyn Barker, Melanie's predecessor, who helped me find my way round the museum's treasures and is herself the co-author of *A Window on Walton-on-Thames*.

Many Walton people have been good enough to answer my enquiries and favour me with their knowledge or reminiscences of the town. The cricket, tennis and rowing clubs have given me access to accounts of their histories. I should like to thank everyone for their patience and courtesy, especially those who made time for me to come and see them—namely Celia Andrews, Don Andrews, Brenda Charles, David Clark, Betty Crooks, Jennifer Gosney, Ken Griffiths, Jeremy Hall, Fred Lake, Muriel Mason, Helen Mills, Irene Sandells, Ronald Segal, Alice Sharp, Timothy Sedgley, Brian Turner, Paul Vanson and Jo Wainwright. The material they gave me was of enormous value, and any misuse of it is my responsibility alone.

# Illustrations

The great majority of the illustrations in this book are in the collection of the Elmbridge Museum and appear with their permission. Authority for the use of other pictures comes from the following, to whom I am most grateful: Brenda Charles and Betty Crooks, 149; Jennifer Gosney, 121-2; Jeremy Hall, 26, 29, 47, 118, 125, 128, 134-7; Fred Lake, 89; Muriel Mason, 143-4; the *Surrey Herald*, 130; Walton Cricket Club, 150; Walton and Weybridge Amateur Operatic Society, 147-8; and Valerie Williamson, 86-8, 90.

*To Barbara*
*as we approach forty years in Walton*

# *Introduction*

An atlas of England lists more than 20 places called Walton, two of them in Surrey. This is the story of one of these, Walton-on-Thames, on the south bank of the river between Kingston and Staines, some 17 miles west of London. It traces the town's past as far as the 1970s, when Walton joined with neighbouring communities to form the present-day borough of Elmbridge.

Walton's first known appearance in a written record is in Domesday Book, as Waletone, but there is archaeological evidence of habitation long before, which is not surprising, as the town lies at a natural crossroads. From west to east flows the Thames, one of the country's main navigable rivers, still tidal at Walton until the 19th century. And since there was a ford nearby the people of Walton had access to the north bank and control of a crossing-point between Middlesex and Surrey.

Much of Walton's history has lain in the development of these east-west and north-south links. In the days before proper roads the Thames was the highway linking the string of royal palaces which lie along it from Greenwich to Windsor: the stretch through Walton was especially important between 1540 and 1650 when the monarch would hold court at Oatlands Palace or Hampton Court. The needs of 17th-century commerce saw the ford across the Thames replaced by a ferry service, which in the 18th century proved inadequate enough for a local businessman to finance the first bridge. In the 19th century the London–Southampton railway replaced the Thames as Walton's east-west artery, and also dictated the character of the town. It never became dependent on light industry (as did many places of similar size when agriculture declined) but offered a convenient home to people with interests in London, whose houses and estates provided local employment. In the 20th century the north-south link acquired a new importance after the opening of Heathrow, with regular traffic jams forming at the river crossing.

Evolution from Saxon hamlet to Thameside village to commuter town has affected Walton in two ways. One is a conscious local identity, with a determination that the needs of the town should be respected by those whose primary interest is in travelling through it to London or commuting by car across the bridge. The threat to the town's character which was posed by the loss of a number of notable buildings to development brought a Walton Society into being in 1975. Since then the society has successfully challenged the traditional political parties in the majority of Walton seats on the Elmbridge Council.

The second Walton characteristic is a sense of the town's history, seen in the many street names which commemorate or echo the past. To take a few examples: Ashley Road, Cottimore Lane, Felix Road, The Grove, Holly Avenue and Oakfields all recall large houses which have disappeared; The Chestnuts, Grange Court and Manor Road relate to houses which still exist; New Zealand Avenue marks Walton's particular role in the First World War; Dale Road, Fairfax Close, Hepworth Way, Rodney Road, Sidney Road and Stonebanks are named after people or families with a place in Walton's history, and Misty's Field from a much-loved horse whose pasture made way for development. Many of these people and places occur in the pages which follow.

**1**   Walton viewed from the air in the 1920s. To the left of the picture are the open grounds of Ashley Park, while the new roads off Terrace Road (top right) still stop well short of the river.

# One

# Early Days

> Caesar, of course, had a little place in Walton—a camp or entrenchment or something of that sort. Caesar was a regular up-river man. Also Queen Elizabeth, she was there too. You can never get away from that woman, go where you will. Cromwell and Bradshaw (not the guide man, but the King Charles's head man) likewise sojourned here. They must have been quite a pleasant little party, altogether.
>
> J.K. Jerome, *Three Men in a Boat* (1889)

Julius Caesar was the first big name in British history. His possible association with Walton dates from his second campaign in 54 B.C. when his aim was to inflict a military defeat on the Catuvellauni, the British tribe most hostile to Rome. Their stronghold was in present-day Hertfordshire, and according to Caesar's account in his *Gallic Wars* he first entered their territory by crossing the Thames at a point some 80 miles from the sea. The British had fortified the river with rows of sharpened stakes, some of them below the waterline, and the Roman infantry (wading shoulder-high) needed cavalry support to force a passage. Supporting the theory that this encounter took place at Walton are the facts that there was a ford there; the distance from Caesar's landing point in Thanet is approximately right; and stakes have been found in the river on the Halliford bend (by the eastern end of the present Desborough Channel).

In 1586 William Camden, an antiquary and historian, located the crossing at Walton and added, ''Tis impossible I should be mistaken in the place, because here the river is scarce six

feet deep, and the place at this day, from these stakes, is called Coway-stakes.' In 1669 John Milton the poet wrote in his *History of England* that Caesar found the Thames 'not passable except in one place, and that difficult, about Coway Stakes near Oatlands, as is conjectured'. In the 18th century William Stukeley published a plan showing 'Caesar's camp at Walton on Thames, August 1st the 54th year before the Christian era'.

Unfortunately these conjectures have a flaw. What is known of the Coway Stakes suggests that there were two rows of them, laid in an arc across the river and probably marking the line of the ford. They would therefore have been more likely to assist an invading legion than to obstruct it. As there is no other evidence of Roman settlement the presence of Caesar at Walton is, at best, not proven.

But even if Caesar did not come by, there are signs around Walton of habitation by other ancient peoples. The large Iron-Age fort on St George's Hill dates from before 100 B.C. Whoever constructed it (and nothing is known of them) would have had a vantage point from which to command the rivers Mole, Thames and Wey. The name of Walton itself suggests an early origin, as the first syllable probably derives from 'Wealh', the Anglo-Saxon word for the Celts. (The same word is the derivation of 'Wales'.) A 'Wealh tun', or Celtic settlement, would be one which predated the Anglo-Saxons' arrival in the country, which took place between the 4th and 6th centuries A.D. The Saxons established the English shire counties, which came to be divided for administrative purposes into groups of parishes called Hundreds. Walton was in the Hundred of Elmbridge, named from the Emele, as the river Mole was known.

The Domesday Survey of 1086 records the apportionment of land after the Norman Conquest. Walton was divided between two manors. One had been awarded to Edward of Salisbury and included three hides (about 350 acres) of land, a mill, a forester, woodland for 50 pigs, 40 acres of meadow, eight villeins, three cottagers and eight bondmen. The other— later known as the Manor of Walton Leigh, as the Leigh family acquired it in the 13th century—also contained three hides of land, together with a church, a mill, a fishery, eight villeins and three cottagers. It belonged to Richard of Tonbridge, who also 'hath 6 hides in the Manor of Absa'(that is, Apps—between Walton and Molesey).

The people of Walton would generally have served their manorial lords either as villeins (serfs) or as free labourers. A villein was required to live on the lord's land and cultivate it. When Aveline de Leghe died in 1298 an inventory of her manor included 11 villeins who had to reap and bind 44 acres of corn, scythe seven acres of meadow and help with the ploughing and carting. She also had 26 free tenants who paid a money rent for strips of land which they farmed for themselves. Their strips would probably have been scattered through Walton's three large open fields: Church Field (south-east of the church, and still commemorated by

Churchfield Road); Sandy Field, beyond Church Field, towards Molesey; and Thames Field, north of the others, adjoining the river. The rest of the area was either communal grazing land, such as Walton Mead in the river bend facing Shepperton, or 'manorial waste' of little value for cultivation.

Serfdom gradually died out in the later Middle Ages as manorial lords preferred money rents to free service and more of their labourers could afford to pay. It is hard to know how prosperous Walton became, but in the early 14th century the community and its leading families proved able to sustain and extend a stone church and to finance the building of a major dwelling, the Old Manor House. This suggests a degree of local wealth. Even more significant was the crown's grant of a licence in 1516 for two annual fairs, one at Easter and the other in early October, each of two days' duration. Fairs were important trading concessions, and Walton's right to hold them would not merely have conferred an advantage over the villages around but probably showed that influence was passing from the manorial landlords to the local merchants and river traders.

By the time the fairs began one of the two Walton manors had reverted to the crown. The Manor of Walton-on-Thames (the location of which is not known) passed to an heiress, Margaret de Bohun, and formed part of her dowry when she married Henry Bolingbroke in 1380. She died in 1394, and five years later he seized the throne as Henry IV. The Manor of Walton Leigh, which was then centred on the Old Manor House, remained with the Leigh family until 1537. In that year Henry VIII required Giles Leigh to exchange it for some land which had belonged to the Hospital of Savoy 'lying near the King's manor of Hanworth'. This transaction was one of many whereby Henry acquired all the manors between the rivers Mole and Wey so as to create a huge new hunting park. At the western end of this estate he built his new palace of

**2**  An early print of St Mary's Church, showing the main (west) front and also the north door, which was bricked up in the 1750s when the Shannon memorial was installed.

**3**  Walton's other medieval building, the Old Manor House. The print's original caption called it 'President Bradshaw's house', enshrining the local legend that it belonged to John Bradshaw, president of the court which tried and sentenced Charles I.

Oatlands, and most of the rest became the Hampton Court Honour, or Chase.

The Chase was subject to forest law, designed to protect deer and their hunters. Some farming was still allowed, but there were limitations on the building of fences to protect crops and on the ownership of dogs, as well as ferocious penalties for poaching. Local people complained, but with no success until after Henry's death in 1547. Then the Privy Council, giving as their reason the cost of maintaining the Chase, dismantled it and removed the deer to Windsor. Though the Chase must have damaged Walton and its commerce in the short term, the long-term effects of royal interest were probably beneficial. Elizabeth I and her two successors held court at Oatlands, and in James I's reign the building of Ashley House and of new galleries in the church are evidence of Walton's development.

Charles I came to Oatlands within a few months of the start of the Civil War in August 1642. It was briefly his headquarters after his advance on London was repulsed at Turnham Green. Walton's parish register records the burial in November of 'a Captain among the Cavaleirs with his boy'. But soon the king's forces withdrew northwards and westwards, and Surrey remained in Parliament's hands for the rest of the war. Walton's leading citizens seem anyway to have been Parliamentarians. Benjamin Weston, of Ashley House, and Francis Drake, the current lord of the manor who lived at Walton Grove, both sat in Parliament from 1640. Weston served until 1653. Drake was expelled in 1648 when the army dismissed those M.P.s whom they mistrusted (the action known as Pride's Purge) but returned between 1654 and 1659 and also held office as a Commissioner of the Peace. Another Walton man, John Inwood, was a captain in the Parliamentary army and helped carry out the survey of former crown property which the Commonwealth undertook in Surrey (as elsewhere) when the war ended.

It may have been Walton's sympathy with the republican cause which led Gerrard Winstanley to choose it for the Digger community which he attempted to set up after Charles I's execution. He argued that, once this event had ended the 'Norman power' which underlay the old system of land tenure, it was open to anyone to take and cultivate the land they needed, so as 'to make the earth a common treasury'. On Sunday 1 April 1649 he and his followers occupied common land on the slopes of St George's Hill. The land belonged to Francis Drake who took no action to stop them; however, the Diggers were infringing the grazing rights of local people who hustled them away and imprisoned them in St Mary's Church. An appeal to a J.P. secured their release. The locals then approached the army. General Fairfax came to see for himself and declined to order any action, reporting to the Council of State that the Diggers posed no threat. But disturbances continued through the summer, and Francis Drake at last took legal proceedings. The Diggers were fined and departed for Cobham, where they stayed another year.

Even though Walton land was refused to the Diggers, much of it was put up for sale in 1649/50 as part of the Commonwealth's drive to raise funds from former royalist property. Oatlands Palace was also pulled down and its effects sold off. Local legend has it that among those buying houses in Walton at around this time were Henry Ireton, Cromwell's son-in-law, and John Bradshaw, who presided at the trial of Charles I. According to a book on Thameside villages published in 1806, Bradshaw lived in the Old Manor House and signed the king's death warrant there. However, there seem to be no contemporary documents linking Bradshaw with Walton apart from a message he sent Fairfax from London, on behalf of the Council of State, instructing him to disperse the Diggers. Bradshaw described them as 'these riotours', suggesting that he had no more patience with popular idealists than with the pretensions of kings.

The years after the Civil War were much calmer for Walton. River trade received a boost with the opening of the Wey Navigation in the 1650s; a ferry to Halliford was established in 1676 and the first bridge to the north bank followed 70 years later. Population also grew steadily. The poll-tax records of 1666 show 474 people living in Walton or in Commonside (the land between the village and the present-day Halfway); a further 240 in Hersham brought the total to 714 for the wider parish. By the 1801 census this had more than doubled to 1,476. One indication of growing numbers and wealth in Walton was the establishment there of an increasing number of inns. The oldest known is the *White Lion*, for which a trade token survives from the 1660s. It stood on the north side of Church Street (the present numbers 23-27) and by 1700, renamed the *White Hart*, it was where the local justices met. Records from 1729 mention the *Bear* (which still exists in Bridge Street, though rebuilt) and also the *Crown*, which occupied the corner of Church Street and High Street. A fourth

inn, the *Castle*, opened a few years later opposite the church. Records from the second half of the 18th century refer to the *Swan*, the *Plough* and the *Duke's Head*, all taverns which survive to this day, if not in their original buildings.

While these establishments show Walton prospering in the 18th century there was concern about the poor. Their relief had been a parish responsibility since 1601, accompanied by a right to levy a poor rate on local property. An Act of 1722 allowed parishes to set up workhouses. From 1732 the Walton Vestry invested £12 a year in renting a group of cottages at Horns Corner (the location of which is not known) to house the poor. In 1769 they undertook the much more ambitious project of building a workhouse, for which over £300 was raised by public subscription. The site chosen was in Ashley Road and is now occupied by The Grange. Various strategies were employed to encourage the poor to meet the

**4**   The *Crown Hotel* stood at the very centre of Walton, on the corner of Church Street and High Street.

**5** The *Swan*, another inn with 18th-century origins, still stands by the river at Walton.

**6** Thames Cottage, on the corner of Thames Street and Manor Road, also dates from the 18th century and still survives.

cost of their keep. A Cobham shoemaker, William Collier, was made workhouse manager in 1772 with a brief to find apprenticeships for poor children. Later a woollen factory was attached to the workhouse (but closed when it ceased to make a profit). In 1792 the average number of inmates was 53, and less than £6 a week was spent on provisions for all of them. But although by the winter the roll had risen to 66 (12 men, 20 women, 17 boys and 17 girls) the Vestry decided they should have 'roast beef and plumb pudding—Mr Young gives the plumbs—for Christmas day'. So ended the last year of peace before the Napoleonic Wars.

# Two

# The River and the Bridges

Walton's name has long been linked to the river. It appears as Waleton super Thamse in the Assize records of 1229. An early Thames traveller from London to Windsor would have found Walton set back from the river (as it still is) and clustered round the church which stands on Bishops Hill. A little beyond the village the Thames was joined by a tributary, the Engine River, flowing out through what are now the backwater and the marina. The meadow of Cowey Sale lay between the Engine River and the Thames. Early maps show Cowey Sale as belonging to Middlesex, not Surrey; only beyond it did the county boundary turn north to rejoin the Thames. Both this and the fact that the Engine River was sometimes called 'Old Thames' suggest that the main river may once have followed a more southerly course.

Cowey was originally Cow-way (a cow path) and Sale is probably from sallow, a willow tree. Long before there was any question of bridging the Thames a Cowey Bridge across the Engine River linked Walton village to Cowey Sale. Beyond the Sale, where the Thames turned right towards Shepperton and Weybridge (there was no Desborough Cut until the 1930s), Walton's ford was marked by the Cowey Stakes which showed where cattle could be driven across the channel. The settlement on the north bank was (and is) called Halliford— probably designating a Holy Ford maintained by the monks of Chertsey Abbey. The abbey, founded in 666 by St Erconwald, stood at the next natural crossing above Walton and was a dominant local presence until the 16th century.

In the ninth and tenth centuries Viking ships came up-stream to attack both Chertsey Abbey and Staines. After the Norman Conquest the crown assumed control of four 'royal rivers', including the Thames. It assured their upkeep in return for the income from tolls and manorial rights. Crown ownership lasted until Richard I,

**7**  John Stonebanks (1903-86), the local historian who did much to establish that the Cowey Stakes were probably a river crossing rather than a line of defence. He is seen here by Walton's city post, which was placed on the bridge to mark the limit of the City's jurisdiction over coal shipments into London, and which still stands.

7

who sold his jurisdiction over the Thames to the City of London in return for much-needed funds. Meanwhile there was enough riverside activity at Walton in the 11th century for a fishery to be recorded in Domesday Book. This may well have been a fish weir, a frame of woven willow in which fish were trapped. Such weirs were controversial, being regarded as obstructions to navigation and harmful to fishing elsewhere. They were outlawed by Richard I in 1197 and again, soon afterwards, in Magna Carta. But they persisted. A Walton man, Richard Clark, was summonsed for using one in 1386. Over 100 years later a document of Henry VII complained that, 'The frye and brode of fishe in grete multitude have been taken by the fishers with unlawful ingynes and nets'. (The word 'ingyne' for a fish weir may have given the Engine River its name.) A fiercer dispute over fishing rights arose in 1521 when an action by Giles Leigh against a number of Walton fishermen was set down for hearing before the King's Bench, withdrawn, and then made the subject of a petition to Cardinal Wolsey. But the outcome is not known.

The river was a trade route as well as a fishery, and by the 15th century Walton was sufficiently busy to have its own wharf. A wharf keeper, James Mason, was appointed in 1485. Oatlands Palace was built in 1540 (largely with material taken from Chertsey Abbey) and the demands of its royal residents must have boosted river traffic further. By 1592 the state of the towpath at Walton and Apps was causing sufficient complaint for the Privy Council to accuse the townspeople of negligence and require them to repair it. Between 1602 and 1607 Walton's own grand mansion, Ashley House, was erected, and we know that vast quantities of building material arrived by river and were unloaded at the wharf: the records survive. But the rise in commerce did not end the importance of fishing rights. Charles I transferred those between Shepperton and Walton to his queen, and when in 1640 she sought to pass them on to Anthony Goddard,

one of her footmen, the City Corporation objected—one of the increasing number of quarrels between the royal couple and their subjects.

In 1676, after the Civil War, a licence was granted for a public ferry between Walton and Halliford, suitable to carry a horse and cart or a coach. Its first operator was Sir William Boreman, a steward of Charles II. The ferry departed from Thames Street, which then extended to the river. It lessened the journey time to London by enabling Walton people to use the roads north of the Thames, which were better than those in Surrey and steadily improved in the interests of the court at Windsor. Its drawback was its unreliability, especially, it appears, the unwillingness of the ferrymen to run any service in the early morning. Among those who resented this inconvenience was Samuel Dicker, a business-man with plantations in Jamaica, who came to Walton around 1744. He proposed a bridge across the river, offering to finance it himself in return for charging a toll.

Local reaction was hostile. Walton Vestry foresaw undesirables crossing into the parish from the far shore. Fishermen and ferrymen argued that a bridge would harm their liveli-hoods, and bargees saw problems in navigating through narrow arches. Dicker went ahead with a petition to Parliament, which legislated in 1747 to allow a bridge to be built; the Act met some of the worries about navigation by stipu-lating that it must have a high, wide central arch. William Etheridge designed the bridge and oversaw its construction. It was a wooden structure based on three stone piers, and opened in 1750 to general acclaim for its elegance. Canaletto painted it. Dicker was proud enough of his achievement to claim that a bridge of best timber 'will last for a space of at least 200 years without repairs'.

Samuel Dicker died in 1760, and his bridge outlived him. But serious repairs were soon necessary. In 1780 his nephew and heir, Michael Dicker Sanders, sought parliamentary

**8** The first Walton bridge, depicted in a print of 1752. It was fashionable to ride out and admire Samuel Dicker's construction.

**9** The second Walton bridge. An engraving by J.C. Varrall dated 1830, based on a drawing by J.M.W. Turner and showing the view from the north bank, with the Cowey Bridge (left) leading away to Walton village.

permission to increase the tolls and thereby finance the replacement of the three wooden arches by four of brick. This second bridge was designed by James Paine, who also designed the Thames bridges at Chertsey, Richmond and Kew. Like its predecessor it was praised for its appearance, attracting the attention of the artist J.M.W. Turner. It lasted about twice as long.

Despite ferries and bridges over the Thames, most of Walton's trade still went up and down the river rather than across it. The importance of Thames traffic is illustrated by the exemption of watermen from impressment into the army or navy: in 1712 this immunity was granted to John Shirly, a Walton man who shipped goods to London. By 1746 there was a timetable for services on the river. Walton boats left London's Queenhithe wharf and Hungerford Stairs on Tuesdays, Thursdays and Saturdays in summer, Tuesdays and Fridays in winter. In 1770 the City's Navigation Committee commissioned a survey by James Brindley, the canal engineer, of the river between Boulter's Lock and Mortlake. He proposed construction of about a dozen locks. Nothing was done until the turn of the century when bargemen registered a series of complaints that some stretches of river, including Ballinger's weir below Walton, were too shallow for vessels with the standard draught of 3ft. 10in. to avoid grounding. At the worst point, near Halliford, the depth could be as little as 2ft. 8in. in a dry summer, and up to 12 horses were needed to drag the bigger barges over the shoals. Locks were therefore commissioned at Shepperton and Sunbury, both opening in 1812. A direct

navigation channel from Weybridge to Walton was also proposed, but the idea lapsed when the Duke of York, George III's second son and landlord of Oatlands, asked for greater compensation for his land rights than the City was prepared to pay.

Early on the morning of 11 August 1859 cracks appeared in the carriageway of Walton Bridge. Mount Felix, close to the bridge and the former home of Samuel Dicker, was then occupied by Herbert Ingram, founder of the *Illustrated London News*. A writer in that publication described what happened next:

> I had crossed the river, just below the bridge in a punt with a friend, to take a sketch of it from the Walton side when the falling of a few stones from the broken arch warned us to quicken our speed. Before we had well reached the shore, the pier suddenly gave way and the large arches on either side fell into the river with a tremendous crash. The water splashed up like a fountain and the sudden displacement caused the river to rise in a wave four or five feet high, which, rolling down the stream carried boats, punts, logs of timber and everything within reach before it'.

**10**   Horses fording the river, as sketched by Lady Mary Bennet, daughter of the 4th Lord Tankerville. Lady Mary was born in the 1780s and lived at Felix Mount, as Mount Felix was then known, until her marriage in 1831.

**11** Sunbury Lock opened in 1812, with its lock house on the Surrey bank and therefore in Walton parish.

For several years there was no bridge at Walton, and ferries were resumed. The vagaries of these were shown while Russell Sturgis, an American banker with Baring Brothers, was renting Mount Felix from the Ingram family. Sturgis was driving his coach-and-four off the ferry on the Walton side when the boatman allowed it to drift away from the bank. At one point the front two horses were on dry land, the rear two in the water, and the coach still aboard the ferry. It took considerable skill on Sturgis's part to complete the crossing safely.

The third Walton Bridge was built in 1863-4. It was designed by E.T. Murray as a flat iron girder construction, with four spans on solid piers. It began the tradition of ugly bridges at Walton. Like its predecessors it was at first privately owned, and maintained by the tolls which its owner was allowed to collect. However, an Act of 1869 made all Thames bridges toll-free and required the riverside counties to maintain them. In Walton's case this caused an immediate dispute. Surrey claimed that, as Cowey Sale was in Middlesex, both ends of the bridge stood on Middlesex land; Middlesex argued that the river formed the county boundary and the costs of the bridge should therefore be shared. A first attempt to settle the matter at law was abandoned because all the judges were found to be Middlesex

**12**   The third Walton bridge, photographed around 1920 with a Salters steamer passing through and sailing boats in the background.

residents. It was eventually decided in 1877 on neutral ground in Kent, at a two-day hearing in Maidstone. Sources as far back as Caesar's *Gallic Wars* were adduced in court as evidence of where the historic boundary ran, and the *Surrey Advertiser* of the day commented:

> It is curious that a question of legal liability arising at this day should turn a good deal—indeed entirely—on the locality of a spot described by Caesar, mentioned by Bede, and carefully identified by Camden.

An expert in geology was called to give his view on the course and width of the Thames at the time when the two counties were designated in King Alfred's day. The court's eventual ruling was that the bridge and its southern approach, including the old Cowey Bridge, should be treated as a single span with each county maintaining half of it. This outcome left Cowey Bridge as a Surrey responsibility but put the whole of the river bridge into Middlesex, in effect a verdict in Surrey's favour.

By now the City Corporation's jurisdiction over the upper Thames had ended and the new Thames Conservancy, formed in 1866, had taken control. Steam power had also arrived. A regular service of saloon boats, taking a day from Kingston to Windsor and another two days on to Oxford, was operating by 1882. In his *Dictionary of the Thames* Charles Dickens, the novelist's son, berated steam craft for their speed and their disregard of other river folk—anglers, oarsmen and boating parties—and concluded, 'the average steam launch engineer is an unmitigated nuisance'. Sometimes their misdeeds were punished. A Mr A.E. Edwards who, one Sunday in May 1895, steered his launch 'without special care and caution' while passing other vessels at Walton was fined £2 the following month.

The Three Men in their Boat were ambivalent about steam launches. They condemned them as roundly as Dickens on a first encounter, but changed their minds when given a tow up-stream by a friendly one. The three men (and their dog) were not the only fictional visitors to Walton's river at the end of the 19th century. In H.G. Wells' account of *The War of the Worlds* the narrator was in Weybridge when a wounded Martian with a heat-ray fell into the Thames and turned it scalding hot; he escaped by stealing an abandoned boat and paddling it on a tide of hot water down to Walton Bridge.

**13**  Sailing boats alongside the *Anglers*.

**14**  *Above.* The Walton regatta of 1908.

**15**  *Right.* A view across the river of the *Anglers*, the *Swan* and Clark's boathouse. There is a punt in the foreground. According to Louise Bale of the *Swan*, 'The river was very good for punts in Walton reach, very shallow from Sunbury weir up to Rosewell's boathouse'.

In 1862 the first regatta was held on the straight stretch of river below Walton known as the Walton Mile. Before long this became an annual event. In her memoir of the 1890s Miss V.E. Connolly, later a local headmistress, recalled how the grounds of Mount Felix were opened to the public and 'young men played banjos, old men accordions, boys mouth organs, children waved flags and babies rattles ... For one day in the year Walton went continental'.

For a few years from 1894 the focus of the regatta moved downstream from Mount Felix to River House, which was rented by Sir Arthur Sullivan. A military band was engaged to provide the music (including Sullivan's own). On at least one occasion Sir Arthur had with him his collaborator, W.S. Gilbert, and Richard D'Oyly Carte, who staged their operas at his Savoy Theatre and who had recently built himself an island house at Weybridge. But Miss Connolly was not impressed. According to her recollection,

As near the tow path as they could get were three men: the one in the middle was beautifully dressed and wore a grey bowler; on his right was a large old man in very old, unpressed clothes and wearing a black bowler; on his left was a queer figure, a very small old man, wearing a voluminous black cape which gave him a clerical appearance, enhanced by the large floppy black felt hat he sported. He wore black glasses. The word went around that this was d'Oyley Carte [sic] from his island fortress outside Shepperton and with him two of the greatest celebrities of those days, W.S. Gilbert and Arthur Sullivan ... I was bitterly disillusioned. They didn't care one jot for the racing.

Gilbert never uttered a word. Sullivan grumbled like a querulous old woman. I pitied d'Oyley Carte but I needn't have bothered. They were a gold mine to him'.

Another composer who visited Walton's river was Jerome Kern, who called at the *Swan* when on a boating holiday with two friends. There was a piano in the pub parlour and the landlord's daughter, Eva Leale, later said of that first visit, 'I never heard such piano playing in my life'. That was in 1909. Jerome and Eva were married in St Mary's Church in October 1910 and lived briefly in Manor Road before leaving for New York and Hollywood. The Bale family, who took over the *Swan* the following year, made sure that it maintained a bridal suite.

In the early 20th century much of Walton's entertainment centred on the river. There were two riverside taverns besides the *Swan*: the *Anglers* next door, which was first licensed in 1870, having previously been a private house called Angler's Cottage, and the *Weir Hotel* near Sunbury Lock. There were two boatyards: Clark's alongside the *Swan* and Rosewell's a little upstream, between the backwater and the bridge. Both firms built skiffs, punts and larger boats, hired them out and offered instruction in navigation. Both also made swimming lessons available, as the river was popular for bathing. A Swimming Club was

formed, which eventually moved into its own purpose-built premises, with changing rooms and diving board. The Walton Rowing Club followed in 1927, opening the way for local oarsmen to compete at Henley and elsewhere. There was also a large and popular camp-site, while Cowey Sale became (and still is) a venue for visiting fairs. Recollections of the turn of the century include the circus coming to town, with the animals, including elephants, arriving by barge and being led through the streets from Walton Wharf. In the 1930s a private zoo was opened at Brownacres (on what became Desborough Island) but closed when war began.

Another feature of the Thames until the 1930s was occasional serious flooding. The greatest was in 1894, when punting was possible along the roadway between Walton and Chertsey bridges. Walter Broomfield, who later emigrated to New Zealand, left a description of that flood and its aftermath:

**16**  *Left.* Rosewell's boathouse, seen across the entrance to the backwater. The bridge carrying the towpath was variously known as the iron bridge or the horse bridge.

**17**  *Below.* Walton Swimming Club's bathing pavilion.

**18**   Walton's riverside tented campsite, downstream from the village towards the *Weir Hotel*.

Late in the autumn, the Thames was in flood, 14 feet 3 inches above the summer level at Walton on Thames ... 6 feet of water on the road just beyond Walton Bridge, then when the floods had receded on December 26th, frost set in and in Walton 14 weeks of frost, the Thames frozen over for 7 weeks, no traffic, ice 6 inches thick in the middle of the river, skating up the river as far as Windsor and to Hampton Court downwards, then about the 3rd week in March an ox was roasted on the Towpath near the Iron Bridge leading to the Back Water lake.

Another big flood at new year 1924/5 led the *Surrey Herald* to report that on one day

the river was a mile wide. Between those dates Louise Bale, whose father was landlord of the *Swan* from 1911, recalled that in some winters

> There were planks to walk on between the *Swan* and the *Anglers*, they had water right up to their bar doors. The boatman once took my sister and I in a boat right over the hedges of the meadows across the river, it was very exciting and a bit frightening.

Flooding was eventually controlled when the narrow winding course of the Thames between Weybridge and Walton was enhanced by a wider, deeper direct channel. This was under-

**19**  The river in flood at the end of 1924. It reached its fullest extent ('a mile across' according to the local paper) on Tuesday 30 December.

**20**  The third and fourth Walton bridges, which stood side by side from the 1950s till the 1980s.

**21**  The fourth bridge was not at all picturesque, but for its first ten years offered an excellent view of Mount Felix.

taken in 1930 so that the river's commercial traffic, which was still considerable, would be able to bypass the Halliford bends. The work took five years: in 1935 the new cut was opened by Lord Desborough, chairman of the Thames Conservancy, and named after him. It had both the intended effect of speeding up the shipping and the useful side-effect of containing the water of the Thames in winter, so that it no longer burst its banks at Walton.

In the Second World War the need to keep fuel supplies safe from enemy action led to the construction of a pipeline across the country from Avonmouth. It terminated in a storage depot by the river at Walton, entered from Sunbury Lane and blocking off River Walk. At first the fuel continued down-river to London by barge, but in 1943 the pipeline was extended to Kent and used to service the D-Day landings. The terminal in Walton was retained, and later became a peacetime depot for Shell.

Another legacy of the war was bomb damage to Walton Bridge. It was declared unsafe for traffic, and a Bailey bridge—of military design and intended to be temporary—was built alongside it, taking all its traffic from 1953. The earlier bridge (Walton's third) was finally pulled down in 1985. By then the fourth (Bailey) bridge was also showing signs of wear, with weight restrictions to protect it from the heaviest vehicles. The following year Surrey County Council tabled proposals for its replacement by a four-lane bridge for motor vehicles, with a separate suspension bridge for pedestrians and cycles. Local reaction was cool. Though the new plans were much more visually attractive than the third and fourth bridges, their

**22** A view downstream towards Sunbury church, showing some of the river's commercial traffic.

promise of increased traffic flow into an already congested town was far less welcome. A prolonged debate over the dimensions and capacity of the fifth Walton bridge had begun.

In the post-war years there were several developments which enhanced the riverside. The Rowing Club opened its new headquarters at Sunbury Lane in 1953. In the 1970s the Elmbridge Leisure Centre was built downstream from the town. Meanwhile a large marina for motor cruisers, developed from the existing backwater and approached from the river

through a new high arch, opened in 1969. But these initiatives did not prevent Walton from gradually turning its back on the river. Commercial traffic all but ended. Salters Steamers ceased to call. The town's indoor pool removed the attraction of river bathing. The camp-site closed, and the hiring of punts and rowing-boats dwindled away. Though the Rowing Club, the regatta and many cabin cruisers still put it to good use, the Thames which was once Walton's high road became instead the town's attractive backwater.

# Three

# A Thousand Years of St Mary's

Walton's parish church stands on a small rise a few hundred yards from the Thames. Before modern buildings arose it would have been visible from much of the present parish and from a long stretch of river. It is a very old foundation. The earliest part of the present structure is Norman architecture of the 12th century, while Domesday Book confirms that there was already a church at Walton by 1086.

There is no evidence of how much earlier it may have been founded, but a possible clue is offered by the theory that in some early churches a lodestone (which acted as a primitive compass) was used to establish the building's east-west axis. If this technique was adopted at Walton a calculation has shown that the orientation of the church would have coincided with magnetic east around A.D. 700 (and not again

**23**  St Mary's viewed from Church Walk.

before 1300 or so). An eighth-century foundation, though entirely speculative, would fit in with the establishment of Chertsey Abbey and the interest of its monks in the Holy Ford.

Features of the church which can be dated to around 1150 are the stone columns in the north aisle and a part of the north wall. The next oldest part of the building appears to be the chancel, which is 14th century. A small part of the east window is also of this date: its wording carries (in Latin) a simple lesson on the existence of the Trinity. The south aisle is in a perpendicular style which dates it to the 1370s or later. It includes the chapel of All Saints, where a pillar is marked with three votive crosses, such as were sometimes left by pilgrims bound for Canterbury. The present church tower was probably added around 1450, but may have replaced an earlier one.

The ancient parish of Walton-on-Thames was very large. It embraced modern Hersham and Burwood Park and extended to Painshill and almost to Wisley. The first rector of Walton of whom we know is Richard Stapulford who disputed with Chertsey Abbey in 1227 over some tithes from Ottershaw. At that time the rectory rights belonged to the Manor of Walton Leigh, whose lord enjoyed the tithe income and appointed the rector. But around 1374 Thomas Leigh sold the rectory rights. By 1413 these had been acquired by Henry Bowet, Archbishop of York, who used them to endow a chantry of All Hallows in York Minster. Two priests of the chantry administered the parish of Walton, collecting its tithes and returning a fixed annual sum of £20 13s. 1½d. of which £12 was a vicar's salary. The appointment of the vicar became a matter for the chantry at York.

This arrangement continued until chantries were abolished in 1548 and the crown took over Walton's rectorial rights. The right to collect tithe income and the financial obligations which went with it (including the payment of the vicar's £12 stipend) passed to the occupier of the Parsonage, a house also known as Walton Grove. The appointment of the vicar remained with the crown. These changes marked the formal transfer of St Mary's from the Roman Catholic faith to the new Anglican communion. However, the religious ambivalence of the time is illustrated by the quatrain which is printed on a pillar close to the pulpit: it is said to have been composed by Princess Elizabeth before she became queen and to express her beliefs in a form which would be acceptable to Catholic and Protestant alike:

> Christ was the Worde and spake it
> He took the bread and brake it
> And what the Worde doth make it
> That I believe and take it.

An incident of Elizabeth I's reign is recorded in the church by the Selwyn Brass. This first shows John Selwyn, Gentleman Keeper of the Royal Park of Oatlands, standing with his wife Susan and 11 children, and next depicts him killing a stag after jumping onto its back, a feat which he performed in the queen's presence. The brass also records that Selwyn died in 1587, and that his five sons and six daughters all survived him. His widow remarried and had three more children.

On their visits to Oatlands Palace Elizabeth and her successors were accompanied by a large train of courtiers, which meant larger congregations at Walton. Accordingly new west and north galleries were added to the church early in the 17th century. The roof was raised to provide space for them: in the absence of local stone, brick was used to build up the walls. The earliest of the church's present peal of bells carry the dates 1606, 1608 and 1610. Another, slightly later, acquisition was a Scold's Bridle dated 1633 and inscribed:

> Chester presents Walton with a bridle
> To curb women's tongues that talk too idle.

One of the wealthiest men in Walton in the late 16th century was Edward Chester, and it was long thought that a member of his family donated the bridle after losing a legacy through malicious gossip. But around 1970 the same verse couplet was found in the parish records of a church in Cheshire. This raises the possibility that it was the city of Chester which sent the bridle to Walton, although the circumstances in which that may have happened remain a mystery.

Leonard Cooke, who became Walton's vicar in 1633, remained at the church through the upheavals of the Civil War. In 1643, soon after an ordinance which banned 'monuments of superstition and idolatory', he and his congregation had to fend off a group of 'military saints' who came to denounce the observance of the sabbath as Jewish and ceremonial. Refused admittance to the church, the saints burned a bible in the churchyard. Early in 1649 (the year of the Diggers' brief imprisonment in the church) several soldiers entered an evening service and demanded to take over the pulpit, from which to deliver a message direct from Almighty God. Again, the vicar and congregation refused. After a long argument the soldiers withdrew to the churchyard and lit four candles there, extinguishing them in turn as a sign of the abolition of the sabbath, tithes, the clergy and the bible. The prevailing Puritanism did not prevent the hanging of a fourth bell in St Mary's tower in 1651. But it did allow church weddings to be solemnised by laymen. Three such ceremonies are recorded for 1654: two of them were conducted by Francis Drake, the M.P. and local landowner who had been a reluctant opponent of the Diggers.

At the time of the restoration of the monarchy Walton's vicar was David Anderson, but he left (or was expelled) in 1662, just before the Act of Uniformity came into force. The following year William Lilly became one of Walton's churchwardens. Lilly, who lived in Hersham, was a nationally known astrologer, whose predictions had caused him to be arrested by—and rewarded by—both sides in the Civil War. Subsequently he foretold the Great Fire of London and was briefly imprisoned again on suspicion of having made good his prophesy by starting it. To Walton he was a benefactor,

THIS Engraving is a facsimile of the Scold's Bridle, which is still to be seen in the Vestry of Walton-on-Thames Church. The date of the presentation is 1632, and the inscription runs thus :—
          "Chester presents Walton with a bridle,
          To curb women's tongues that talk too idle."
The tradition respecting this Bridle—one of the few and oldest examples yet remaining in England—is, that a person named Chester gave it to Walton Parish, because he had lost an estate " through the instrumentality of a gossiping, lying woman."

Harold Smith's Emporium, Walton-on-Thames.

**24**   An engraving of the Scold's Bridle, made when it was 'still to be seen'. It was stolen in 1965.

writing, 'I settled as well as I could the affairs of that distracted parish, upon my own charges.' He died in 1681, and a floor plaque marks his burial place in the chancel.

The fortunes of the church revived in the new century. A survey of church livings in 1705 records the provision of a 'vicarage house' by wealthy parishioners. In 1711 St Mary's acquired the organ which Bernard Smith, Charles II's Organ Maker, had built for the king's private chapel at Windsor Castle in 1673. In 1726 the church received another gift as John Palmer, the High Sheriff of Surrey who lived at Walton Grove, presented the tower with a fifth bell. This proved more controversial. In 1728 the Vestry formally resolved that Palmer

had set up chimes without the knowledge or
consent of the parish, and declined to maintain
them. It is not clear how the issue was resolved,
although a later gift from Mrs Frances Palmer,
another member of the family, had a friendlier
reception. Following the Jacobite invasion of
1745 she presented a loyal banner to the church
to mark her 'opposition to the present unnatural
Rebellion' and the parish put a flagstaff on the
tower from which to fly it.

The church's 18th-century memorials
include several to members of the Rodney
family who occupied the house by the river
later known as Mount Felix. There is also a
house in Church Street (number 17) called
Admiral Rodney House on the basis that
George Brydges Rodney, the future naval hero,
was born there in 1719. However, there is no
sure evidence of this, or of the admiral's
retaining any connection with Walton during
the career which led to his triumph at All Saints
in 1782. The church nevertheless sought to
celebrate the 150th anniversary of that victory

**25**  Roubiliac's memorial to Lord Shannon. The field
marshal is standing with a weeping figure to his left
hand and weaponry on his right.

in 1932 by flying the White Ensign from the
tower; they swiftly received official instructions
to take it down, on the grounds that St Mary's
was neither a naval vessel nor a ship of the
Royal Yacht Squadron.

A military man who was not lost to
Walton was Richard Boyle, 2nd Viscount
Shannon, who owned Ashley House and whose
baroque memorial is the largest in the church.
Shannon had a 50-year army career, serving as
a 15-year-old volunteer at the Boyne in 1690
and dying as a field marshal in 1740. He fought
with distinction in Marlborough's wars but saw
no military action thereafter: in the words of
his memorial inscription, 'During a long and
continued Peace he attained by Royal Regard
and just Favour what he was ambitious to
achieve by Service'. His widow, who died in
1755, left £1,000 for a memorial to him, and
the commissioning of it fell to their daughter
Grace, Countess of Middlesex.

The Countess's plans to honour her father
on a grand scale came before the Walton Vestry
the following year. A first meeting to consider
it was inconclusive, but a second resolved, 'the
Monument cannot be erected without the
gravest Inconvenience to the Inhabitants of this
Parish as it not only tends to Darken it ... and
possibly to Damage the Church, but will like-
wise ... take up space sufficient to Accommodate
at least twelve people at a time when Several
Persons of Distinction are making great
complaints' of lack of room. The conclusion
was, 'We judge that we cannot in Justice to
ourselves or Posterity agree to the erecting of
it and do Absolutely Refuse.'

Lady Middlesex's supporters included
Samuel Hughes, the vicar, and they fought back.
By 1758 they had got their way. Though the
north door had to be bricked up to accommo-
date it, the church acquired an impressive work
by Louis François Roubiliac, a leading sculptor
of the day whose other works include General
Wade's memorial in Westminster Abbey and
Newton's statue at Trinity College, Cambridge.
Roubiliac's design allows for one figure of grief

(presumably representing Lady Shannon or Lady Middlesex) who is shown clasping an urn, but otherwise focuses on presenting Lord Shannon in military mode. He appears life-size in uniform, standing outside his field headquarters. To his left are barrels and drums, and to his right, alongside a gunbarrel and a dozen cannon balls, is a field gun with a curved barrel (for the sake of perspective) trained on the congregation.

The rifts in the parish caused by the memorial dispute took time to heal. There was a six-year gap in the Vestry minutes after 1756, and a five-year delay in the collection of a church rate. The vicar's nominee for one of the churchwarden posts was rejected by the parish. A smaller, but possibly connected, unpleasantness arose in 1762 when the bell-ringers condemned George Betney, a church-warden, as 'a Jacobite' for his meanness in refusing them five shillings for a victory peal to celebrate the capture of Havana in the Seven Years' War. Their anger was fiercer because Quebec had been regarded as worth six shillings three years before.

By the 1770s sufficient harmony had returned to the church for a third, south gallery to be built. It was approached by a staircase from the south door, which may well have been a 'squire's door' linked by Church Alley (now Church Walk) to a point in the High Street which faced an entrance gate to Ashley House. We know that early in the 19th century the eastern ends of both aisles were occupied by Ashley pews. The practice of reserving pews for leading houses and families was a useful source of church income, but had the draw-back of restricting room for other worshippers. This had featured in the dispute over the Shannon memorial and probably contributed to the decision to provide extra places for worship in a chapel-of-ease at Hersham, which was established in 1839. But there was another factor: Hersham had become a local centre of nonconformity and an Anglican presence was felt to be needed there. In 1851 the Hersham

26  A 19th-century print of the church pulpit.

chapel became the church of a separate parish, and Walton's parish boundaries were redrawn along, very nearly, their present lines. The process was completed with the building of St Mary's, Oatlands, in 1862 and the designation of its parish in 1869. However, these changes only affected matters of worship. The Walton Vestry retained civil jurisdiction over the whole of the ancient parish until its powers were trans-ferred to the new Urban District in 1894.

In 1851 a religious census took place, with the size of the congregation in every place of worship being counted on Sunday 30 March. There were morning and afternoon services at St Mary's on that day. In the morning there were 197 adults present and 85 Sunday scholars (45 boys and 40 girls). In the afternoon the general congregation was 177 and the Sunday school registered 66 (36 boys and 30 girls). There is no way of telling how many of these people were the same on each occasion. The census also recorded the average size of the congregation over the previous 12 months, and 171 was the figure for St Mary's.

**27**   The 18th-century vicarage which stood next to the church on the site now occupied by Regnolruf Court.

Walton's vicar between 1816 and 1851 was Thomas Hatch. There is a memorial in the church to him and his wife Anna, and four more commemorating other members of his family. Around 1830 Mr Hatch found the vicarage next-door to the church no longer fit to live in, and left it for several years while rebuilding work took place. Later, in 1847, he acquired an additional small property off Manor Road (which may explain the presence of a Vicarage Walk in that area). In the 1851 census Mr Hatch is recorded as living in the original vicarage again, and after his death that year his Manor Road holding was bought by a local butcher, Harry Mayo Dale. Mr Dale had come to Walton in the 1840s, and in 1880 offered himself for election as churchwarden. However there was another candidate, a Mr Careless. After a show of hands appeared to favour his opponent the Dale supporters demanded a poll, which was held on Thursday 8 April with voting between 10 a.m. and 8 p.m. Both candidates canvassed support with printed election notices: Mr Dale's presented him as an 'Old and Tried (but not found wanting) CANDIDATE who has Proved himself a Thorough Churchman for double 20 years'. Despite this the outcome was a win for Careless—121 votes to 61.

In 1883 three more bells were added to the church's peal to give the present total of eight. The opportunity was taken for the bells to be rehung. Four years later the ringers received a gratuity of five shillings (little improvement on a century before) for a three-hour peal to mark Queen Victoria's Golden Jubilee. In 1902 the present pulpit was installed as a gift to the church from Mrs Fanny Gill, the last owner of Apps Court, in memory of her husband and daughter. The same year, on the initiative of a new vicar, Walter Kemp Bussell (who had been appointed in 1901 and was to stay 30 years), the parish took the decision to build a church hall. Its foundation stone was laid in May 1903, and work was completed in time for an official opening before Christmas by the Duchess of Albany, King Edward VII's sister-in-law, whose home was at Claremont in Esher.

The First World War is commemorated by two memorials in the church: one for 117 local men killed in action and the other for 21 New Zealanders (including one woman, a nurse) who died at Mount Felix while it was a military hospital and who are buried at Walton. It was decided to mark the peace with a new baptistry, which was consecrated in 1924. The south gallery was pulled down to make way for it, and the font moved from the north to the south aisle. In 1927 a change of a different kind saw Walton parish, historically in the diocese of Winchester, transferred into the new see of Guildford, though it was more than

another 30 years before Guildford, now a bishopric, also became a cathedral town.

The 1930s brought electric lighting to the church: it was installed in 1935 (after 70 years of gas). In 1936 the present church organ replaced the former one, which was more than 250 years old and on which Sir Arthur Sullivan had played during his lease of River House in the 1890s. The condition of the 18th-century vicarage was also causing concern, and it was decided to replace it. A plot was secured in the new Ashley Park development and a house built there in 1938 to a design by Charles Mole, one of the churchwardens who was also an architect of note. Some parishioners were surprised at the location of a new vicarage so far from the church, and a few ascribed the decision to move across town to a tradition that the previous building was haunted. Once empty, the old vicarage was bought by a developer named Furlonger who demolished it and built a block of flats which, reversing his name, he called Regnolruf Court.

**28**   The interior of St Mary's. This photograph is datable to the early 20th century as it shows both the present pulpit, which was donated to the church in 1902, and the south gallery, taken down around 1924.

**29** Gladys Ward (1887-1976) tending an Easter garden in the All Saints chapel at St Mary's. Miss Ward, who lived in Highfield Road, came to Walton at age 12 and left recollections of growing up in the town. Above her is a memorial to Alison Jardine (mother of England's cricket captain, D.R. Jardine), who died in 1936.

In the Second World War the church suffered fire damage in two separate bombing raids, in March 1941 and early in 1944. Each time the church's 'fire-watchers' had to contain the blaze until the brigade arrived. The south aisle lost its roof and had to be covered by a tarpaulin until repairs were possible, but only one service was cancelled. In June 1944 the flying bomb which fell on Bridge Street caused further damage, and extensive renovations were needed at the end of the war. These included a replacement for the flag pole, broken in the bombing, and it was decided to mark the events which led St Mary's to erect its past and present flagstaffs by inscribing on the weather vane the dates 1745 and 1945.

The new pole was fashioned from a tree trunk presented by Eva Drabble, previously of the Grange, from the garden of her new house, Birdswood, in Ashley Park. Mrs Drabble was associated with the church all her life: she was married there, gave two windows as family memorials, and is commemorated by the altar rail in the All Saints chapel. Her principal gift to St Mary's was a plot of land in The Furrows on which a daughter church could be built. She donated this in 1939, a year after fortnightly services began at Ambleside infants school for the benefit of the new housing in that area. Fundraising for a church building on the new site was put on hold in wartime, but resumed in 1945. Eight years later the resources were available for work on the structure to begin. The architect was the same Charles Mole (now Sir Charles) who designed the pre-war vicarage. By the end of 1953 the church in The Furrows was ready; it was consecrated in December, and Walton's ancient parish of St Mary acquired the additional protection of St John.

*Four*

# Houses and Estates

## Apps Court

The name of Apps appears in records long before that of Walton. It was part of the lands given in 675 to his newly founded abbey at Chertsey by St Erconwald, then Bishop of London. Indeed, the Rev. W. Kemp Bussell, vicar of Walton in the early 20th century, wrote of a Christian settlement at Apps even before the foundation of Chertsey, but it is not clear what his evidence was for this. Apps is mentioned in Domesday Book as owned by Richard of Tonbridge, who also held the manor of Walton Leigh. Richard appears to have enlarged Walton Leigh at the expense of Apps, which was administered from another of his manors at Stoke D'Abernon. There is no record of anyone at Apps, which lay close to Molesey and therefore at the very edge of Walton, exercising manorial rights elsewhere in the parish.

Walton people nevertheless enjoyed a charitable endowment at Apps, recorded as early as 1235. Possibly because the freehold was then held by the crown, the tenant of Apps was obliged to provide alms every year on All Souls Day for the benefit of the king's soul. These consisted of a quantity of bread and ale, and a pig worth 12d. Though the requirement for a pig was lost at some stage, the annual distribution of beer and bread lasted for almost 800 years. The local importance of Apps was also shown in 1332 when its lord (not named, but probably a family called Brocas) had to pay 7s. in tax, the highest assessment in Walton.

In the 15th century the Agmondisham family acquired Apps. They ceded it to the crown to form part of the Hampton Court Chase, recovered it in 1548, and immediately sold it again. In 1578 it was the property of Thomas Thorne, and four men from West Molesey were convicted at Surrey Assizes when they broke in, 'destroyed his herbage and committed other enormities'. In the tax assessment of 1593/4 Apps was again the highest-rated property in Walton, valued at £10 and rendering its owner liable to a £2 payment. In 1602 it was bought by Francis Leigh.

James I made Leigh a baronet, and when the new king, Charles I, raised a loan from his better-off subjects 'Sir Fra Lee of Aps Cort Kt and Bart' offered £40 (the second highest payment in Surrey). He died in 1625 and his son, also called Francis, was made Lord Dunsmore three years later. In 1639 Dunsmore received royal permission to divert local roads and enclose Apps as a private deer park, and in 1644 was created Earl of Chichester. Early the following year he served as one of the king's representatives at the Uxbridge Conference, an attempt brokered by the Scots to end the Civil War in a negotiated peace. The conference failed, and Chichester soon had to come to terms with the victorious Commonwealth. An Act of 1650 allowed him to keep Apps but required him to live there under house arrest. He paid Parliament a fine of almost £3,000, and died in 1653.

Apps remained in the family of the Earl of Chichester and by 1664 was occupied by his granddaughter, Elizabeth, and her husband, Lord Percy. Local records for the Hearth Tax (levied from 1662 on dwellings valued at £1 or more) refer to a house with 39 chimney-hearths. But the Percys spent more time in London than Walton: in 1667 Lady Percy caught the eye of Samuel Pepys, who called her 'a beautiful lady indeed'. The property was soon leased out. An early tenant was Bernard Granville, a friend of John Evelyn the diarist. Evelyn records visiting him in 1673 'at Abs-Court in Surrey, an old house in a pretty park'.

In the 18th century the heirs of Lady Percy sold Apps Court, and by the 1740s it was owned by a local man, Jeremiah Brown. In 1778 it was occupied by his grandson, Jeremiah Hodges, who commanded the Surrey militia. This was the year in which France and Spain entered the American colonists' war against Britain; an invasion might be expected, and Hodges wrote despairingly to the Secretary at War that his

was 'the only Regiment ... in the Kingdom unprovided with Pouches and Buff accoutrements' and further that 'our Arms are extremely bad, & our Cartridge boxes unfit for service'. From the Hodges family Apps passed to John Hamborough, who in 1824 pulled down the old house and built a smaller one 'in white brick with a noble stone portico supported on Ionic columns'. In 1854 it was bought by Robert Gill, a former railway engineer, whose business interests included membership of the group which bought the Crystal Palace and moved it from Hyde Park to Sydenham.

Gill died in 1871 and his widow Fanny became the last private owner of Apps. Even in her day the ancient tradition of a distribution of beer and bread on All Souls Day was still carried on. According to a newspaper report from 1892, a large crowd assembled at 5 a.m.

**30**  Apps Court, as rebuilt by John Hamborough in 1824, photographed in the 1880s.

on a Sunday morning in a field adjoining Mrs Gill's residence. They brought 'cans, jugs and even buckets' in which to collect their beer, and after this was distributed a horse and cart drove round the field and loaves were thrown out to them. A much earlier, 17th-century account of the charity estimated that 200 or 300 people took advantage of it each year.

In 1898 Fanny Gill sold her house and land to the Southwark and Vauxhall Water Company. Apps Court disappeared into the Knights and Bessborough reservoirs. The disappearance of charitable bread and beer caused an outcry on the next All Souls Day: a crowd gathered at the former entrance to the house demanding, 'Where's our beer?', and the police were called to control them. There was a petition to the Charity Commissioners, who responded by requiring the water company to make a payment of £200 (now held by Walton Charities) to absolve the debt. Thereafter, instead of a fashionable house on the edge of town, Apps became (in the words of Gladys Ward, whose recollections were recorded in mid-century) 'a dirty part of Walton with bargees'. An *Apps Court Tavern* survived until the 1960s. Apps Court Farm, which was the home farm of the old manor and separated it from the river, remains to perpetuate the name.

## The Old Manor House

St Mary's Church and the Old Manor House are Walton's two medieval buildings. The house, which retains its original structure and timber frame, can be dated accurately to the early 14th century. Though no records of it survive from that time, a very similar building ten miles away, Staines Hall, is known to have arisen in 1327, and expert opinion is that the same group of craftsmen worked at both sites. The Manor House would have been built for the Leigh family, who occupied it for the next 200 years.

In 1537 Giles Leigh accepted the king's offer of land away from Walton in return for the inclusion of his manor in the Hampton Court Chase (see p.2). When the Chase was discontinued the Old Manor House remained crown property and was leased out. Before long it was primarily a farm. In a survey which the Commonwealth commissioned in 1649 it was called Lemon's Farm, and in 1650 it was part of the crown land sold for £1,521 to John Smith of London. This transaction hardly seems consistent with the local legend of John Bradshaw's ownership, although Smith (from whom the crown recovered its property in 1660) could have been an agent for Bradshaw.

A generation later local folklore links the Old Manor House with Judge Jeffries, the Chief Justice who passed fearsome sentences on rebels against James II; however, there is no documentary evidence of his presence. In 1779 the house was still a farm. A survey of that year records that Dr Richard Palmer leased it from the crown, that it stood in 11 acres of land, with a large barn and a pond which abutted on Thames Street, and carried with it a further 75 acres in Thames Field, Church Field and Thames Mead. This substantial farming interest seems to have lasted until land tenure was reorganised under the Inclosure Act of 1800, when separate farmhouses for these outlying parts of the estate were built at New Farm (off Manor Road) and at Sull Farm, which has survived as the present Thames Field Farm.

By 1871 the Old Manor House had declined from a working farm to a tenement. In that year's census it appears as five dwellings occupied by six labouring families, comprising 36 people. A writer of the time describes the house as squalid and delapidated, with occupants who were miserably poor. By 1881 multi-occupation of the house had ended: it was the home of John Rosewell, a fisherman, his wife and nine children, and a lodger. However, the area around the Old Manor House remained very run-down. The cottages in nearby Manor Place were known locally as the Rookery, a Victorian word for slum.

In 1890 Lowther Bridger bought the freehold of the house from the Fitzroy Investment Association. While he did not live there (but

**31** The Old Manor House, photographed early in the 20th century while still in a run-down state.

**32** Manor Place in 1961, with the Old Manor House in the background.

elsewhere in Manor Road, at Elmbank) he began its restoration, proposing at one point that the new Urban District Council might take it over as offices; his offer was refused. His successor, G.M. Weekley, who owned the house between 1912 and 1937, contemplated its conversion into a marmalade factory, but this plan was also abandoned. It took time for the antiquity and value of the Old Manor House to be fully appreciated. When Admiral Wilson bought it in 1957 it was listed as a Grade II property and thought to date from around 1500.

In 1963 the house was sold again. The new owner was Ronald Segal, an exile from his native South Africa following his editorship of *Africa South*, a magazine opposed to the apartheid regime. (The ban upon his return to South Africa was lifted only in 1992.) He obtained expert advice on the house's origins, with the result that its 14th-century date was established and authenticated and its listing raised to Grade I, a rarity for a building still in use as a family home. Restoration work was also completed and the Manor Place cottages pulled down, revealing a fine view of the house from Manor Road. Later, in 1987, the Old Manor House played a small part in history when Ronald Segal hosted a meeting there between Oliver Tambo and Thabo Mbeki, of the African National Congress, and Chris Ball, head of Barclays Bank in South Africa. This contact helped convince Mr Ball that business must cease supporting the apartheid government and work instead for its replacement by a democratic alternative—as happened, to world-wide acclaim, seven years later.

## Walton Grove

A property with a history as long as the Old Manor House was the Parsonage, later known as Walton Grove. It stood outside the town towards Apps Court—in modern terms, on land between Cottimore Lane and Sandy Lane. It may originally have been the rector's home, but ceased to be so when Walton's rectorial rights were sold off at the end of the 14th century. Once these rights were acquired by a chantry at York Minster the tenant of the Parsonage seems to have acted for the chantry in collecting tithes and meeting certain church expenses such as the vicar's £12 stipend.

These arrangements largely survived the abolition of the chantry in 1548. The owner of the Parsonage continued to be entitled to tithe income, with which a tithe farm was eventually established; in return he had to keep up the fixed annual payments of £20 or so which the chantry had made and also maintain the chancel at St Mary's and in the parish church of West Molesey. The right to collect tithes lasted until the 19th century and the financial obligations to the church until 1935, when the Church Commissioners remitted them in return for a single down-payment into ecclesiastical funds.

Shortly before their chantry was abolished the priests at York granted a long lease of the Parsonage to John and Joyce Carleton. This was honoured by the crown and the Carletons occupied the house until their tenancy expired in 1583. The following year Richard Drake took over the estate, which remained in his family for 170 years. Richard's grandson, Francis Drake, was the lord of the manor who played a leading role in Walton during the Civil War and the Commonwealth. After the Restoration he moved to Woodstock in Oxfordshire and the Parsonage was let. Its tenant from 1663 was the Duchess of Somerset. A tax return of 1669 records that the house had 21 hearths, and in 1710 crown permission was obtained to demolish it and put up a smaller modern property. During much of the 18th century it was occupied by the Palmer family. At the

same time the Drakes retained the right to Walton's tithe income and an interest in the Parsonage land. These were eventually vested in Francis Drake's great-granddaughter Adria, who in 1739 married Denton Boate.

Adria Boate was widowed in 1754, and seems to have expected remarriage to Christopher D'Oyly, a barrister of the Inner Temple. She died only a few months after her husband, and by then had willed D'Oyly all her estate. D'Oyly came to live in Walton; he married 10 years later. Along with his wife Sarah he is commemorated in St Mary's church, where an inscription describes him as 'a man of clear discernment and sound judgement, equally distinguished for unsullied integrity as for the exercise of every social virtue'. Christopher D'Oyly died in 1795, and Sarah in 1821 at the age of 96. During her widowhood Sarah D'Oyly was awarded 64 acres of common land under the Inclosure provisions, but she put these up for sale and also sold her rectorial rights to Walton's tithe income.

The Parsonage, now called Walton Grove, passed through various hands in the early 19th century before being bought by Paul Cababe, a lawyer born in Aleppo, Syria. He substantially rebuilt and extended the house, with embellishments to the ironwork which included a Lion of Judah and a Star of David. He also added what one local memoir called 'a lovely little chapel lodge on Terrace Road with Hebrew lettering'. Soon after coming to Walton Paul Cababe brought an action against a Mr Peachey for damage which his brougham, valued at £175, suffered in a traffic accident. Much later his widow Marianne went to law in a far bigger way, as her dispute with the local authority over the maintenance of Cottimore Lane reached the High Court in 1914. The Court found in Mrs Cababe's favour and the Urban District had to accept responsibility for the work.

Paul and Marianne are among eight members of the Cababe family buried in Walton cemetery. Another is their nephew Michael

**33** Walton Grove, as rebuilt on a massive scale for the Cababe family. Increasingly hemmed in by other housing, it stood until 1973.

who inherited the Grove when Marianne died in 1915. For a couple of seasons from 1926 he loaned a field off Terrace Road to Walton Football Club, then searching for a permanent home. After his death in 1933 his widow Amelia sold the house and 35 acres to Allan Ansell for development. Walton Grove was soon surrounded by other properties and converted into flats. It eventually became very run-down and, given its age and size, could not easily be restored. The Council bought it for demolition in 1973.

**Ashley Park**

A hundred years ago there were shops (as now) on the east side of Walton's High Street, but most of the west side was a plain wall—'a lovely rose red wall' according to someone who remembered it—in which was set one of the entrances to Ashley Park and its grounds. This private estate covered the land now occupied by New Zealand Avenue, Ashley Park Avenue and Silverdale Avenue, stretching back alongside Ashley Road almost as far as the railway. A property comparable in size to Apps Court but much closer to the town, it was Walton's principal residence for more than 300 years.

A building at Ashley is first recorded around 1550. It was leased by the crown to Roger Yonge, keeper of the king's game at Oatlands. After his death in 1586 the lease (which still had 40 years to run) was acquired by Sir Michael Stanhope on behalf of his sister, Lady Berkeley. From 1602 Yonge's modest house was replaced by a far grander one which included a hall, great chamber and gallery as well as numerous lesser rooms. It cost over £3,000 and took five years to build. But Lady Berkeley only retained the property until 1611. The lease was sold on to further tenants before reverting to the crown in 1626.

Ashley House was then awarded to Christopher Villiers, Earl of Anglesey, younger brother of the king's favourite, the Duke of Buckingham. Anglesey was appointed steward of Hampton Court but died in 1630. Six years later his widow married Benjamin Weston, who became an M.P. in 1640 and remained a Parliamentarian throughout the Civil War and Commonwealth. There is a legend that he was close enough to the leadership for Cromwell to have stayed with him at Ashley House; this is unproved but possible. Certainly he was trusted enough to be allowed to offer asylum to his elder brother Jerome, Earl of Portland, who had been at Charles I's court at Oxford between 1643 and 1646. Portland was fined some £5,000 by Parliament, and then allowed to join Benjamin at Ashley House. Benjamin later sold the house to Portland (probably when his wife died in 1662) and Portland died there the following spring. A commemorative stone marks his burial place in St Mary's Church.

**34** High Street early in the 20th century, showing the wall of Ashley Park. Halfway along is one of the entrances to the house and grounds.

The 1664 Hearth Tax records list Ashley House (25 hearths) as the property of Charles, Earl of Portland, Jerome's son. But in 1665 he was killed at Lowestoft in a sea battle against the Dutch and left the house to his mother, the Dowager Countess. Around 1670 she leased it to Matthew Andrewes of the East India Company, whom the king knighted aboard a Company ship in 1675 and who later became an M.P. and a colleague of Pepys as an Elder Brother of Trinity House. Sir Matthew seems to have been extremely quarrelsome: in his time at Walton he is recorded as disputing the repair costs of Ashley House with Lady Portland, wrangling with the Duchess of Somerset over the burial of one of her servants in the church, arguing with the Vestry over the position of the pulpit, and denouncing William Lilly as a 'rogue and rascally traitor'.

Ashley House was sold after Lady Portland's death in 1694, and 20 years later came into the hands of Richard Boyle, Lord Shannon, the soldier whose memorial stands in St Mary's. Shannon had the house considerably rebuilt, adding a new wing and turning the long gallery into a ballroom. His interests were not solely military; there is evidence that he invited Alexander Pope to visit Ashley House while the playwright Congreve was staying there. His heir was his daughter Grace, who married the Earl of Middlesex, a friend of Frederick, Prince of Wales. Grace Middlesex became Mistress of the Robes to Frederick's wife Augusta in 1745. Horace Walpole described her as 'very plain' and as 'a vain girl, full of Greek and Latin, and music and painting; but neither mischievous nor political'. In the 1750s she won the battle to give St Mary's a worthy memorial to her father, but she died childless in 1763. Ashley House was inherited by various cousins in quick succession before passing in 1786 to Sir Henry Fletcher, the first of four baronets of that name who occupied it until the 1860s.

The first Sir Henry was at Ashley House in 1800 when Walton's Inclosure Act was passed. He took advantage of it to double the size of the estate, acquiring much of the common land which lay south of Stompond Lane, between the Hersham and Ashley roads. About this time Ashley House began to be known as Ashley Park, and its main entrance was moved from the High Street to a point close to where Ashley Park Avenue now joins Ashley Road. Sir Henry also bought a property towards the river called Great Romers, to become the dower house for Ashley Park. Renamed Ashley Cottage, it survives as 9-13 Oatlands Drive.

The second Sir Henry lived quietly in Walton. The third Sir Henry was active locally, especially in charitable work for the poor. He and his wife Emma suffered the tragedy of losing three of their children in a single week in 1845 and gave St Mary's its font in their memory. The fourth Sir Henry was still at school when he inherited the title in 1851. He retained Ashley Park until 1863 when it was bought for £48,500 by Sassoon David Sassoon, a Jewish businessman who had come to London from Bombay to run a branch of his family trading company. Four years later Sassoon died at the age of only 35, leaving a widow Flora and a young family.

Flora Sassoon ran the house and estate until her son Joseph came of age in 1876, an event she celebrated by endowing Walton with a village hall in the High Street (on the corner of Churchfield Road). However, her daughter and second son were banished from the house for marrying outside the Jewish faith. As a result her grandson Siegfried Sassoon, the war poet, never came to Ashley Park while his family owned it; he visited it only later, when calling on his friend E.M. Forster in Weybridge. Joseph Sassoon, who made a marriage his mother approved of, inherited the house and brought up his seven children there. The household was generally very self-contained, with parents and children basing their family entertainments on the notion that their home constituted the Republic of Ashlesia, of which Arthur Read, Joseph's longstanding secretary and friend, was

**35**   Ashley Park, the main frontage, which could be seen distantly from the estate's principal entrance in Ashley Road.

**36**   Ashley Park, the back of the house seen across the gardens.

**37** The gardens of Ashley Park. This was private land but villagers were admitted (through the High Street gate) to an annual summer fête.

**38** Skating Sassoons. Joseph Sassoon is third in line, with his wife Louise behind him. At the end of the column is Arthur Read, who came to the house as tutor to Joseph's younger brothers and sister and remained as his secretary for more than 40 years.

**39** A cricket party. Arthur Read was the brother of Walter Read, who captained Surrey at cricket and was capped 18 times for England, and leading cricketers accepted invitations to Ashley Park. W.L. Murdoch, who captained Australia, and P.F. Warner, who went on to captain England, both played there, but there appears no basis for the local legend that W.G. Grace did so.

the president. Joseph did, however, become a J.P. and involved himself sufficiently in local affairs that, despite his faith, he was one of the dignitaries present at the formal opening of St Mary's church hall in 1903. He also allowed Walton sportsmen to play on the cricket pitch and nine-hole golf course which he laid out in his grounds.

The cost of maintaining the estate eventually became a burden. In 1907 the golf course, which lay between Stompond Lane and Station Avenue, was sold off for redevelopment, although Joseph Sassoon recompensed club

members with subscriptions to the Burhill course. By 1917 he and his wife Louise could no longer afford to live in Ashley Park and moved to a house called Springfield in Rydens Road. Joseph died in 1918, Louise in 1922, and their eldest son soon afterwards. Executors put the estate up for auction, and the buyers decided to develop the land for luxury housing. The house briefly became a mental hospital, but was pulled down around 1929. Its owner took care to preserve its outstanding architectural features, including a 17th-century staircase which the Westons had installed and

**40** The staircase of Ashley Park, probably dating from its ownership by the Weston family in the 17th century. It was among the furnishings taken to America when the house was pulled down in the 1920s.

Lord Shannon's 18th-century ballroom, and dispatched them to the U.S.A. The cricket ground was recovered for the use of the Walton club. Otherwise the end of Ashley Park as a single estate opened the way for the full re-development of High Street and for much of the residential building of the inter-war years.

**Mount Felix**

From the 1840s until the 1960s the square Italianate tower of Mount Felix would catch the eye of anyone crossing the bridge into Walton or sailing by on the river. The tower was a feature of a long, well-proportioned building which was probably the most elegant in the town.

Mount Felix stood on the slight eminence called Cowey Hill, up-stream from Walton Wharf. It was the fourth building known to have occupied that site. The first was Still House, owned in the 1680s by Elizabeth and Anthony Twine; Elizabeth was the daughter of John Inwood who surveyed crown property in Surrey at the end of the Civil War. In 1713 Harry Rodney, father of the admiral, bought Still House, rebuilt it, and sold it to a family called Smelt. In 1744 it was sold again to Samuel Dicker, the builder of the first Walton Bridge. Dicker acquired all the riverside between the wharf and his new bridge, and laid out a lawn and terrace. He also built onto the house. But it did not win the same plaudits for its appearance that his bridge did: a history of Surrey records that 'the residence was a large edifice of no architectural pretensions whatever'.

The house was sold on Dicker's death in 1760 and for most of the next decade was occupied by John Zephaniah Holwell, the former Governor of Bengal who brought home the news of the Black Hole of Calcutta. (According to Holwell's account, throughout one night in 1756 almost 150 people were imprisoned in a dungeon in Fort William, Calcutta, and he was one of only 23 who came out alive.) Holwell left Walton in 1769, and the house was purchased by Charles Bennet, 4th Earl of Tankerville, in 1772. Lord Tankerville's enthusiasm was cricket. He employed as his head gardener Edward 'Lumpey' Stevens who was a leading Surrey player, and the next summer captained a team from the county which played the Duke of Dorset's Kent team at the duke's estate at Knole and won. Stevens, then in his late forties, was in that winning team. Stevens's main claim to cricketing fame was that, three times in a match against Hambledon, he had bowled a ball between the stumps of the then two-stump wicket but, because the bail was not dislodged, had not dismissed the batsman. In 1774, the year after the Kent *vs* Surrey fixture, a committee which included the Duke of Dorset and Lord Tankerville ruled that a wicket should have three stumps.

In 1789 the Duke of Dorset was British ambassador to France and invited Lord Tankerville to bring a team to Paris to play a French side. The earl agreed, but when he and his fellow-cricketers reached Dover they met the duke retreating to London after the fall of the Bastille. The match was accordingly postponed for 200 years. In 1989, as part of the bicentennial celebrations of the Revolution, the French invited the M.C.C. to complete the fixture. It was played in the Bois du Boulogne, and France won by seven wickets.

Lord Tankerville replaced Dicker's house with a neat two-storey building which he named Felix Mount. He also acquired some additional property, notably Crutchfield House—so named after the family who lived there—together with 10 acres of land and six

**41** Charles Bennet, 4th Earl of Tankerville, bought Samuel Dicker's old property (then known as Walton House) in 1772, rebuilt it as Felix Mount, and lived there for 50 years.

**42**   Mount Felix, the main frontage of the 19th-century house.

**43**   The ornamental gates to Mount Felix which opened onto the approach to Walton Bridge, almost opposite the end of Oatlands Drive.

tenements. (These were presumably the 18th-century cottages which still stand in Crutchfield Lane.) Under the Inclosure Act he was able to add four acres to bring his holding up to the Hersham road. He died in 1822, 50 years after he and his wife Emma had come to Walton. She survived him at Felix Mount for a further 14 years.

The estate then passed to their son, the 5th Earl, who was already 60 years old and a long-serving treasurer of the king's household. He had plans for a grander house and commissioned a design from Charles Barry (later the architect of the Houses of Parliament). Barry's plans, which the earl adopted, were for a large mansion in the Italian style. It was built between 1837 and 1840 and its name reversed to Mount Felix. As part of the alterations a palm house had to be demolished. One of the palms

was about 50 feet high, and the earl agreed to let the Duke of Devonshire have it for his new conservatory at Chatsworth. Joseph Paxton came to Walton to negotiate removal and transport, and the tree trundled north on a specially constructed wagon, pulled by up to 11 horses. Some toll gates had to be dismantled to let it through.

In 1852 the earl retired to his London house and sold Mount Felix. In 1856 it was bought by Herbert Ingram of the *Illustrated London News*. Ingram was drowned only four years later: he was visiting the U.S.A. and involved in a steam-ship accident on Lake Erie. His widow Ann remained at Mount Felix (remarrying at age 80) and died there in 1896. The new owner was John Cook, son of Thomas Cook the travel agent. Cook's time at Mount Felix was active: he had Walton's first telephone

**44** Royalty at Mount Felix. The value to the mother country of New Zealand troops crossing the world to fight in France and Gallipoli was recognised by the three leading members of the royal family, King George V, Queen Mary and the Prince of Wales (later Edward VIII) taking tea at Mount Felix within weeks of the hospital opening there.

installed there, opened his lawn for the annual regatta, and gave the town's newly formed Football Club the use of a field for their home matches. But his stay was also brief. In 1898 Thomas Cook & Son arranged a visit to the Holy Land for Kaiser Wilhelm II and Empress Augusta of Germany. John Cook devised the itinerary and accompanied the party. He fell ill in Jerusalem, and died at Mount Felix the following spring.

The house stood empty for several years after Cook's death. In 1905 the trustees of his estate reached agreement with Walton's Urban District Council for its use as municipal offices, library and museum, with public riverside grounds. But in view of its cost to the rate-payers the proposal was put to a local poll, and the voters rejected it by 950 to 239. Between 1907 and 1912 the house was occupied by William Compton, who modernised it and installed a lift. After a further sale it was acquired early in 1914 by a syndicate which planned its conversion into a country club. But war began before this could be carried through, and Mount Felix was requisitioned by the War Office.

After a year of use by British regiments the house was inspected in June 1915 by the New Zealand authorities, who considered it suitable for a military hospital. They installed an operating theatre and facilities for 100 in-patients. Nurses were billeted at the Old Manor House; houses elsewhere in Walton were rented for hospital staff. Mount Felix formally became The Second New Zealand Hospital. (The First Hospital, for more serious cases, was at Brockenhurst.) It was officially opened by the High Commissioner in July 1915 and visited the following month by the king and queen. The initial intake was of men from Gallipoli. The first instance of a patient dying of his wounds came in October, and a funeral with full military honours was held in Walton cemetery.

In January 1916 a hospital extension of four huts, each for 50 patients, was built on the far side of the Walton Bridge approach. Known as Anzac Mount, it was linked to Mount Felix by a footbridge across the roadway. Further huts increased its capacity to 500, but after a year this proved inadequate for the number of casualties arriving from the Western Front, and the *Oatlands Park Hotel* was acquired as a hospital annex. Eventually there were 2,000 beds, and in the whole course of the war some 27,000 New Zealanders were treated in Mount Felix and its extensions. Many of them formed friendships with Walton people as they convalesced and were able to visit the town. Among the marriages which took place was that of Maureen Alderton, of Terrace Road, to Private Peter Poi Poi, a Maori veteran of Gallipoli. Other local people helped the New Zealanders rather over-enthusiastically by giving them access to the alcoholic drink which were forbidden under hospital regulations. One Charles Phillips was sentenced to a month's hard labour for obtaining two pints of beer from the *Old Manor House* pub and smuggling them to a patient at Mount Felix.

On 23 November 1919 a New Zealand banner was formally dedicated at St Mary's and a farewell parade held for the hospital. It finally closed in 1920. Meanwhile the last private owner of Mount Felix had died, and the problem of finding a peacetime use for the estate arose again. Its grounds were gradually sold off for road-widening or development. The land down-river, towards the *Swan*, was acquired by George Miskin, the timber merchant, for a residence called Hillrise. Mount Felix itself was largely turned into apartments, with the ground-floor riverside rooms let out for functions. In 1965 the local authority rejected an application to demolish the building and took it into ownership instead. But the following year, before any redevelopment could begin, a serious fire destroyed much of the house and left the rest unsafe. Despite initial hopes that the tower could be preserved, everything but the coach-house and a few out-buildings had to come down, and Mount Felix now survives only as a geographical name for riverside houses and flats.

**45** Elm Grove, the 18th-century house which still stands where High Street meets Hersham Road. Nicholas of Russia, who stayed there in 1894, described it as 'a cosy cottage'.

## Elm Grove

Elm Grove stands at the southern end of High Street, at the boundary between Walton's old village and the area known until the 19th century as Commonside. It is a square red-brick house which George Shakespeare, an 18th-century architect, designed and built for his own use. On his death in 1797 it was inherited by his niece Mary and her husband, Richard North. The Norths extended their property through the Inclosure awards, and in 1835 the estate passed to their son, the Rev.

William North. After a chapel of ease was founded at Hersham in 1839 William North officiated there for a time, but in the 1851 census he recorded his profession as 'a clergyman without the care of souls'.

William North died in 1859. He had three daughters, and his will required that his estate should be sold to provide for them. The sale did not take place until August 1868 when five properties were auctioned on a single day. These were Elm Grove itself, which stood in 17 acres, Oakfield and The Chestnuts nearby, the Tithe

## S. ROSEWELL, Boat & Punt Builder. Patronised by the Emperor and Empress of Russia, and H.R.H. Prince Louis of Battenberg.

Telephone—
0195 Walton.

All kinds of
**BOATS
FOR HIRE**
By the Day,
Month or Season

New and
Second-Hand
Boats and Punts
always for SALE.

Steam and
Electric Launches
for HIRE.

Commodious
Boat Houses at
Walton Bridge
and
Walton Wharf.

Private Boats
Housed.

**46**   Advertising in Walton's town guide, Rosewell's boatyard made good use of the custom they received from the occupants of Elm Grove, including Nicholas and Alexandra.

Farm and Hersham House. But it seems that Elm Grove cannot have reached the required price, as it remained in the hands of William North's married daughter, Laura Hickley, until her death in 1907.

In the 1890s Mrs Hickley leased Elm Grove to Prince Louis of Battenberg who was then a naval adviser at the War Office and whose wife, Victoria of Hesse, was Queen Victoria's favourite granddaughter. In the summer of 1894 they were visited by Prince Louis' brother Henry and his wife Beatrice (the queen's youngest daughter) and also by Victoria's younger sister Alexandra (Alix). In June the party was joined by Alix's fiancé Nicholas, heir to the Russian throne. According to a letter from Nicholas to his mother he and Alix spent 'three ideal days in [the Battenbergs'] cosy cottage on the Thames ... out all day long in beautiful summer weather, boating up and down the river picnicking on shore for tea'. He concluded, 'I'm delighted by this only too

short stay at Walton.' They left for Windsor and a visit to Alix's grandmother, the queen. Three months later Nicholas's father died suddenly, and he succeeded as Czar of Russia.

After the Battenbergs Elm Grove was leased by the Wilkinson family. One of the six Wilkinson children later wrote of a poltergeist that they encountered there. In 1921 the house was sold to the Urban District Council for their offices. An extension was built to serve as a council chamber and the grounds laid out as a public park with a bowling green and tennis courts. The Council remained at Elm Grove when in 1932 the Urban District was enlarged to include Weybridge, and the new authority continued to use it for more than 30 years before moving to a purpose-built town hall. Since then Elm Grove has remained in municipal hands, serving as a courthouse and later being leased to the Stagecoach drama school, but no new civic use for it has been devised.

*Five*

# Nineteenth–century Village

At the end of the 18th century Walton was still a village of five streets. Church Street was the main thoroughfare. High Street led southwards to Elm Grove and Commonside. Alongside it, a few yards short of the *Plough* inn, stood the village pound in which stray horses and other animals were kept until their owners paid to redeem them. From the *Crown*, where Church Street and High Street met, Bridge Street ran north to the river crossing. Thames Street led off Bridge Street and met the river near the *Swan* and the town wharf. From there Back Street (sometimes called Back Lane, and now Manor Road) looped round to the village, coming out opposite the church and the vicarage. Some 1,500 people lived in Walton parish as a whole, about 1,000 of them in the village and Commonside.

As in medieval times the villagers of Walton held parcels of land in the open common fields nearby. Beyond these there seem to have been five established farms. Apps Court Farm was the home farm of the Apps estate. Closer to the village was the Tithe Farm, part of the estate of Walton Grove. Between the Tithe Farm and Apps Court were Fishmore Farm (towards the river) and Crown Farm (further inland). Most of this land now lies beneath the Queen Elizabeth II Reservoir. Beyond Crown Farm was Field Farm at present-day Fieldcommon. A further 2,800 acres of surrounding land, uncultivated and largely scrub, was known as Walton Common. This was 'manorial waste', not in common ownership but the property of local manors. The tenants

of those manors had the right to graze their animals on the Common and collect fuel there, which prevented it from being brought into cultivation and put to productive use.

In view of the pressure which population growth and (from 1793) prolonged war with France was putting on the national food supply, Parliament began to enact measures to allow common land to be enclosed and redistributed, thereby opening it up for farming. In 1799 the lords of the manor in Walton and the surrounding areas petitioned for local Acts which would allow such a development in Surrey. The Walton Vestry opposed the initiative, and tried to rally support from the Duke of York, who owned Oatlands Park, and from neighbouring parishes—but without success. In 1800 Parliament passed 'An Act for dividing, allotting, and inclosing, the Open Common Fields, Meadows, Pastures, Commons and Waste Lands in the Parish of Walton upon Thames and the Manor of Walton Leigh in the County of Surrey'.

Under the Act three Inclosure Commissioners were appointed to survey the land, apportion it according to the previous rights which individuals had held in the common fields, and sell the balance. Anyone awarded a new holding, generally in place of strips dispersed around the village, was required to fence or hedge it. The sale of surplus land paid for the costs of enclosure and the provision of access roads. In practice such land was generally bought by local landlords to consolidate or expand their existing estates. The new arrangements were worked out by 1804 when formal Inclosure Awards were made. These had four main effects: existing landowners enlarged and developed their estates; new farms were laid out; some land was set aside for the benefit of the poor; and improved roads eased the village's isolation.

The principal holders of local land all seem to have done well from enclosure. Across the Weybridge border the Duke of York bought up most of St George's Hill. In Walton, to the west of the present Hersham Road, Sir Henry Fletcher doubled the size of his Ashley Park estate. On the other side of that road an Inclosure Award gave permission as follows for improved access to the principal landholdings:

> We award unto the Rt. Hon. the earl of Tankerville, Richard North and ... Edward Peppin one private carriage road of the width of sixteen feet beginning on the Esher Road opposite Stump pond and continuing along-side the north west side of the allotment of the said Edward Peppin to his inclosure at Walton Lodge.

This drive appears to have followed the line of the present Bowes Road. It was required because Lord Tankerville of Felix Mount had added Crutchfield House to his estate, while Richard North of Elm Grove acquired the land comprising Oakfield and The Chestnuts. As regards Edward Peppin, his original holding at Walton Lodge (broadly where Stuart Avenue now meets Sidney Road) was an early 18th-century house said to have been designed by Vanbrugh. He expanded this by further purchases and briefly became the largest land-owner in Walton, building himself a 'cottage style' villa at Cottimore and a house at Rydens, later known as Holly Lodge and now commemorated by Holly Avenue. He served as sheriff of Surrey from 1802, but after running into financial difficulties sold most of his estate in 1824 and retired to his Rydens home.

The pattern of farming which emerged from the Inclosure Awards allowed the open Thames Field to be divided into Sull Farm (later Thames Field Farm) and New Farm. Two further farms were established towards Molesey

**47** A gatehouse at the end of Crutchfield Lane marked the entrance to Edward Peppin's carriage drive. It still stands. This photograph dates from around 1970.

**48**   Ashley Road was one of the long, straight roads laid out under the Inclosure Act. As Oatlands Drive replaced it in the 1850s as the direct route to Weybridge, it long retained the character of a country lane.

Road, namely Lonesome Farm which came to be owned by the Dale family, the local butchers, and Rydens Farm which developed eventually into Walton Park Nurseries. These four new-comers brought the number of farmsteads in Walton to nine, and the 1831 census gives 'agricultural labourer' as the occupation of 42 per cent of local men.

Though enclosure brought advantages to landowners, farmers and farmworkers it did not benefit everyone. The Act recognised this and required that 200 acres of Walton Common should be allotted in trust for the benefit of 'such poor as are real and true occupiers of cottages within the said parish', poor being defined as paying less than £5 annual rent. The commissioners accordingly designated land, most of it along Seven Hills Road, for this purpose. At first the only use which anyone could make of 'Poor's Land' was to graze animals, cut turf and collect fuel, but an Act of 1832 allowed allotments to be let to 'industrious cottagers of good character'. An Allotments Committee was set up to oversee such arrangements. Its leading figures were the third Sir

Henry Fletcher of Ashley Park and the Rev. William North of Elm Grove. In 1839 they drew up a code of rules covering the annual letting of allotments from Michaelmas and also specifying that 'no occupier shall be suffered to plough his ground, but required to cultivate it by spade husbandry' and that 'any occupier working on a Sunday shall forfeit his land at the end of the year'.

In evidence to a Parliamentary Select Committee Sir Henry justified the limitation to 'spade allotments' as requiring more of a labourer's time than ploughing would do, thus 'inducing him to go to the allotment instead of to the public house'. As for Sunday observance, he and Mr North kept an eye on this in their frequent inspections of the land.

The remaining key aspect of enclosure was that it released funds for the building of roads. The Act laid down that through roads should be 40 feet wide, access roads 30 feet and private farm tracks 15 feet. New main highways were Terrace Road (known as Kingston Road), Hersham Road (known as Esher Road), Ashley Road (known as Weybridge

**49**  Another through route, Rydens Road, appears on the map (as Rydens Lane) as early as 1867. But it was another 60 years before it began to be lined with houses.

Road, as a through route to Weybridge along Oatlands Drive was not available until the 1850s) and Seven Hills Road (known as Common Road). Until these roads were opened the only good land route into Walton was through Middlesex and across the bridge. Now the village stood at a real crossroads, approachable from all points of the compass.

Hardly had road access to Walton been established than the Act to construct a London–Southampton railway was passed in 1834. Its promoters were examined by a House of Lords committee on the new line's impact on estates in its path and, among other reassurances, undertook that Sir Henry Fletcher's water rights would be protected. By 1837 the contract had been let for the stretch of line between Wandsworth and the River Wey. The contractor, Thomas Brassey, had a reputation as a good employer, and there is no record that the presence of several thousand navvies caused

Walton the trouble and disruption which commonly occurred elsewhere. A trial of the rolling stock was observed by Princess Victoria, who visited Hersham a few months before becoming queen and recorded in her diary:

> I saw the steam carriage pass with surprising quickness, striking sparks as it flew along the railroad, enveloped in clouds of smoke & making a loud noise. It is a curious thing indeed.

The line opened in May 1838 between Nine Elms and Woking Common. The inaugural train made the outward journey in 45 minutes and, after a celebratory lunch for the dignitaries present, returned in forty-three. The track to Southampton was completed in 1840 and the line extended into Waterloo in 1848. Walton thus came within an hour's travelling time of London, whereas a journey by coach would take at least twice as long and a boat

**50**  Better roads eventually brought regular public transport to Walton. This photograph from the 1890s shows the *Bear* in Bridge Street, where the Richmond–Windsor coach changed horses at 1 p.m. each day and called again two hours later on its return journey.

# LONDON & SOUTHAMPTON RAILWAY.

The Public are informed, that until further notice, the Trains will start at the following hours, viz.—

| DOWN TRAINS. | | UP TRAINS. | |
|---|---|---|---|
| | Morning. | | Morning. |
| To Winchfield . . . | ½-past 7 | From Winchfield (Mail Train) . | ¾ before 4 |
| To Woking Common . . | 9 | From Woking Common . . | 8 |
| To Winchfield . . . | 10 | From Winchfield (stopping Train) | ¼ past 8 |
| To Winchfield (stopping Train) | 12 | From Winchfield . . . | 12 |
| | Afternoon. | | Afternoon. |
| To Winchfield . . . | 3 | From Winchfield . . . | 3 |
| To Winchfield (stopping Train) | 5 | From Woking Common . . | 5 |
| To Winchfield (Mail Train) . | ½-past 8 | From Winchfield . . . | 7 |

The *Intermediate Stations* from the Terminus at Nine Elms to the Winchfield and Hartley Row Station, are those of Wandsworth, Wimbledon, Kingston, Ditton Marsh, Walton, Weybridge, Woking Common, and Farnborough.

The Trains to and from Woking Common will stop to take up and set down Passengers at the intermediate Stations to the Terminus at Nine Elms, as will also the Train from Winchfield at half-past eight in the morning, and the Trains to Winchfield at twelve at noon, and five in the afternoon.

The Trains to Winchfield at Ten A.M. and Three P.M. and the Trains from Winchfield, at Twelve at Noon, and Three P.M. will stop at Woking Common and Farnborough only.

The Train from Winchfield at Seven P.M. will set down any Passengers who may be booked at Winchfield, Farnborough, or Woking Common for those Stations nearer London.

The Mail Trains will take up and set down Passengers at Kingston, Weybridge, Woking Common, Farnborough, and Winchfield.

## ON SUNDAYS

The Trains will start as follows, and (excepting the Mail Trains) will call at all the intermediate Stations.

| | Morning. | | Morning. |
|---|---|---|---|
| To Winchfield and Hartley-row Station | 10 | From Winchfield and Hartley-row Station (Mail Train) . | ¾ before 4 |
| | Afternoon. | From ditto . . . | ½-past 8 |
| To ditto . . . . | 5 | | Afternoon. |
| To ditto (Mail Train) . | ½ past 8 | From ditto . . . | 5 |

The Servants of the Company are prohibited receiving any fee or gratuity. Private Carriages, Horses, &c. will be conveyed, provided that previous notice be given to ensure accommodation, and provided also that such Carriage, &c. be ready at the Station a quarter of an hour before the departure of the Trains.

**OMNIBUSES** convey Passengers to and from the Station near Vauxhall, from the Spread Eagle, Gracechurch Street; Swan with Two Necks, Lad Lane; Cross Keys, Wood Street; White Horse, Fetter Lane; George and Blue Boar, Holborn; Golden Cross, Charing-cross; and Universal Office, Regent Circus.—Fare 6d.

**STEAM BOATS** convey Passengers to and from the Railroad, from Dyer's Hall Wharf, Upper Thames Street; Hungerford Market, near Charing-cross; Old Swan Stairs, Upper Thames Street; Waterloo Bridge and Westminster Bridge—Fare 4d.

**POST HORSES** are kept at the Station, and Carriages are taken to, or fetched from, any part of London, at a charge of 10s. 6d. including the driver, 2s. 6d.

### FARES.

| Stations. | First Class | | Second Class | | Stations. | First Class | | Second Class | |
|---|---|---|---|---|---|---|---|---|---|
| | s. | d. | s. | d. | | s. | d. | s. | d. |
| London to Wandsworth · · · · · · · · | 1 | 0 | 0 | 6 | London to Weybridge · · · · · · · · | 3 | 6 | 2 | 0 |
| .... Wimbledon · · · · · · · · | 1 | 6 | 1 | 0 | .... Woking Common · · · · · · | 5 | 0 | 3 | 6 |
| .... Kingston · · · · · · · · | 2 | 0 | 1 | 6 | .... Farnborough · · · · · · · · | 7 | 6 | 5 | 0 |
| .... Ditton Marsh · · · · · · · · | 2 | 6 | 1 | 6 | .... Winchfield & Hartley Row | 9 | 0 | 6 | 0 |
| .... Walton · · · · · · · · | 3 | 0 | 2 | 0 | | | | | |

7th January 1839.

**W. REED,** *Secretary.*

Printed by Smith and Ebbs, Tower Hill.

**51**  A notice put out by the London & Southampton Railway eight months after its line opened, when services from London ran as far as Winchfield. It indicates that (apart from special bookings) three trains each way called at Walton on weekdays and two on Sundays.

even more. An inn soon opened for railway travellers, at first known as the *Railway Tavern* and now as the *Halfway House*. But early fares were expensive, and it took time before the opportunities offered by the railway had a wide impact on the village. Its first immediate benefit was to the trustees of the Poor's Land, who owned 10 acres which the railway needed for the line and the station. The company paid £30 an acre. (They would pay more than £300 for an acre of Walton land in 1868, and in 1884 almost £2,000!) The trustees therefore had £300 to invest, and used it to provide poor cottagers with fuel, known as Parish Coal.

Alongside the allotments and the Parish Coal which trustees administered, the principal provision for the poor was still the workhouse. The numbers accommodated in the Grange remained at 70 or 80 throughout the Napoleonic Wars, with a similar number receiving outdoor relief either regularly or occasionally: together these beneficiaries made up about a tenth of Walton's population. In 1834 Poor Relief was reorganised. A workhouse for 250 paupers was established at Chertsey with a Board of Guardians overseeing several parishes, including Walton. The Vestry retained responsibility only for its almshouses and for a group

**52** Walton retained control of these almshouses at the Halfway when most poor relief was transferred to the Chertsey Board of Guardians.

**53**   The Grange was substantially improved on its rebuilding in 1884. Between 1900 and 1930 it was the home of George and Eva Drabble, benefactors of Walton's church and hospital.

of cottages for poor people at Eastonville (the junction of the Terrace, Hurst and Walton Roads, where the *Apps Court Tavern* also stood). The Grange was leased to Sir Richard Frederick of Burwood Park, Hersham, the local baronet who is credited with securing from the railway a bridge at the top of Ashley Road—Sir Richard's Bridge—to maintain his access to his various properties.

As the Chertsey Board of Guardians had responsibility for Walton's poor, two Walton people were appointed to it. One of these was Henry Tilley, a Church Street baker who was also a leading local Methodist. He was among the group who successfully established a chapel in Walton after a long period when opponents of nonconformity had blocked any move to build one. At first the Methodists had bowed to this prejudice and in 1819 founded a chapel in Hersham, rather than Walton. Twenty years later the Congregationalists, similarly denied land in Walton and worshipping in a rented room at the *Bear*, followed their example and built in Hersham. But the Methodists were unwilling to accept their defeat as permanent. In 1844 Joseph Steele, a grocer and ironmonger who was Mr Tilley's neighbour in Church Street,

bought some land off Manor Road as the site for their Walton chapel.

Building rapidly began—so quickly that the Croydon Methodist Circuit found the work was in hand before they had authorised it, and ordered it to be stopped. Mr Steele refused, telling them, 'My neighbours must have the Gospel'. The Circuit gave way, and the new chapel opened on Easter Monday 1845. Joseph Steele gave the land for it, and public subscription of around £400 paid for the building and the furnishings, which included an 'American organ' or harmonium which cost £15 15s. 6d. The religious census of 1851 records that on 30 March that year 55 adults and 39 Sunday scholars attended the chapel for morning service, while 67 adults and 30 scholars were there in the evening. In 1854 the first appointment was made of a full-time minister: this was Thomas Raby, who married Joseph Steele's daughter Elizabeth. (Her older sister Ellen was married to George Brett of Fishmore Farm, whose sister was Mrs Tilley.) In accordance with Methodist practice Mr Raby moved after two years, but he and his wife returned to Walton on retirement and lived on there into the 20th century.

**54** Cottimore was built early in the 19th century, acquired by Thomas Sidney for £3,000 in 1864, later occupied by the Earl of Egmont and finally sold for demolition in 1935. John Stonebanks wrote that Walton thereby lost 'one of its most attractive domestic buildings'.

The general census of 1851 showed that Walton's population had roughly doubled since 1801. It almost doubled again by 1871. This was the period when Walton's large estates began to be broken up for housing development. A prime mover was Thomas Sidney, a former Lord Mayor of London, who acquired the Walton Lodge and Cottimore holdings which had belonged to Edward Peppin. Walton Lodge was pulled down and its grounds made way for the new Sidney Road and Bowes Road. (Bowes Road was named after Sidney's principal home at Bowes Park, Southgate.) Cottimore remained as a large house. A lodge was built for it in Sidney Road, and still survives (number 119). Elsewhere in the village mid-century population growth and prosperity were marked by the opening of several new public houses: the *Ashley Arms* on the Halfway Green, the *Builders Arms* (later the *Kiwi* and now the *Wellington*) in High Street, the *George* in Bridge Street and the *Old Manor House Inn* in Manor Road. There was already a Walton brewery in Bridge Street and a second, the Ashley Brewery, opened off High Street at about this time.

In 1869 the village received two important innovations, a gas supply and piped water.

The second of these made it practicable for a fire brigade, equipped with a hand-pump and a manhandled trolley, to be formed a few years later. But progress was not always welcomed. A press report of 1870 cited Walton as the only village in England still refusing permission for the Government telegraph to erect poles and wires in its streets. Nor was there support for reform of Walton's own charitable arrangements. In theory these were run by a body of trustees which included every £100 landowner in the parish, but in practice many trustees were quite unaware of their responsibilities. Francis Bircham, a solicitor who owned the Burhill estate in Hersham, therefore proposed that management duties should be delegated to a small committee. This caused an outcry, with accusations that Bircham and a few friends were planning to take over the Poor's Land for personal gain. Even when an Act of 1873 required such committees, with between six and twelve members, to be appointed, it was not implemented in Walton. Bircham's principal opponent, another Hersham lawyer named Richard Harris, claimed that he had 'prevented 200 acres of Common at Walton from falling into the hands of the rich' and used this boast

**55** The former lodge to Cottimore House still stands, facing onto Sidney Road, but now hemmed in by other houses and heavy traffic.

**56** The ornamental lake in the Cottimore grounds was fed by a stream from the Stomp Pond (off Hersham Road) which flowed between Bowes Road and Crutchfield Lane. In 1940 the lake was filled in, and the area later became a public park, named in 1962 after George Froude, patron of Walton's sports clubs and four times chairman of the Council.

**57** Walton's gasworks in Manor Road. The gas company bought out the Methodists' original chapel in order to obtain the site.

in his (unsuccessful) attempt to become a local Liberal M.P.

Walton also seems to have had a problem of rowdiness among its growing number of young people. In 1866 three were fined after a Shrove Tuesday game of football in the streets was said to have attracted a crowd of two to three hundred. In 1871 a letter to a local paper claimed that in the early evening 'groups of youths collect round different tradesmen's windows, sing low songs, use disgusting language, and in some cases insult the customers who pass in and out of the shop'. In 1878 the Vestry petitioned for an end to Walton's 350-year-old Easter Fair, as 'it is a great nuisance and causes the congregation of a number of idle and dissolute persons'. An Order in Council duly discontinued the fair the following year. The enthusiasm of Walton citizens could how-ever be harnessed for the celebration of local achievement. In 1870 William Humphries, son of a Walton grocer, won the Queen's Prize for shooting and the National Rifle Association's gold medal. When he returned home he was crowned with laurels and pulled in a carriage through illuminated streets, while a band played 'See the conquering hero comes' and the bells pealed. More sombrely, there was a huge turn-out in 1881 for the funeral of Frederick Atkins, a constable who went to investigate a break-in at a house on Kingston Hill, was shot by the intruder and died the following day. Almost 2,000 metropolitan policemen came to Walton and lined the street between the Atkins home in Commonside (near the *Plough*) and St Mary's Church. There were also Oddfellows in their regalia, as P.C. Atkins had belonged to that Order, members of fire brigades, and a police band. So few pupils attended the village school for their afternoon lessons that it was declared a half-holiday.

Finally, there were at least two residents of 19th-century Walton with a national reputa-tion. Though unrelated, both were called Lewis. John Frederick Lewis, an artist who became a Royal Academician, lived in Ashley Road from 1854. He originally became known for his painting of sporting scenes, and in that capacity George IV required him to live near Windsor in the 1820s. But in 1832 he went abroad to Spain (hence his nickname of 'Spanish' Lewis) and then to Cairo. His paintings began to depict events or narratives with a Mediterranean or Near Eastern setting, and his style foreshadowed the Pre-Raphaelites with its brilliant colours and close attention to detail. John Ruskin praised his large 1856 watercolour 'A Frank Encampment in the Desert of Mount Sinai' as 'among the most wonderful pictures in the world'. He died in 1876, and is commemorated by a plaque in the chancel of St Mary's.

George Henry Lewis, who bought Ashley Cottage (the Ashley Park dower house, which stands in Oatlands Drive) around 1880, had a very different expertise. He was a successful solicitor specialising in cases of fraud and criminal libel, with many celebrities among his clients. One of them, Lillie Langtry, stayed at Ashley Cottage in the early 1880s. Her correspondence with her then lover, Arthur Jones, indicates that Oscar Wilde was another visitor to the house: Jones was jealous of her friendship with Wilde. Later George Lewis acted professionally for Wilde, approaching on his behalf someone who was blackmailing Lord Alfred Douglas and paying him off. However, he did not represent Wilde in his action against Lord Alfred's father, the Marquess of Queensberry, as by then he was Queensberry's personal solicitor as well. He wrote to Wilde, 'Although I cannot act against him, I should not act against you', and tactfully withdrew from the case. Another client and friend, the painter Sir Edward Burne-Jones, wrote that Lewis (who was knighted in 1893) 'knew enough to hang half the Dukes and Duchesses in the kingdom'. Like Wilde and Mrs Langtry, Burne-Jones visited Ashley Cottage, where he painted portraits of Lady Lewis and the Lewis daughters. Writing to the family, he ended a letter with a wish to be in Walton: 'It is much prettier than London' and 'the roses are bigger'.

# Six

# Turn-of-the-century Town

The new century brought a new reign. It also saw Walton change from a village in 1890 to a town by 1920, a transition symbolised by the formation of the Walton Urban District in 1895. In that year elected councils took over many of the services which the Victorians had set up independent boards to run. Walton's new authority inherited responsibility for its roads from the Kingston Highways Board and for public health from the Chertsey Rural Sanitary Authority. It also took on the duties of Walton's Burial Board and Lighting Inspectors. (However, it did not replace the Walton School Board, which remained in being until education became a county responsibility in 1902, nor take back poor relief from the Chertsey Board of Guardians.) In other local matters the Council's authority superseded that of the Vestry.

**58**    A new reign. Church Street decorated to mark the coronation of King Edward VII and Queen Alexandra.

59  Flags out in Manor Road. There were turn-of-the-century celebrations not only for the coronation but also for the Relief of Mafeking and victory in the Boer War.

The last years of the Walton Vestry were not harmonious. Three separate quarrels arose. The first was over who should be entitled to a charitable distribution of Parish Coal. This had long been left to the vicar, the Rev. Thomas McCowan, and two of his churchwardens to decide, but some members of the Vestry committee thought that overmuch preference was being given to retired people of fairly ample means. Accordingly in January 1887 two of them, together with Percy Webb the Vestry clerk, drew out the money for the coal and prepared to allocate it themselves. This led to a fierce argument over both the objectives of Walton charity and who should be allowed to handle the funds for it. In the meantime the distribution of coal was seriously delayed.

The second issue arose when the Highways Board wished to sell a former gravel pit near the station, part of it wanted by the railway company and the rest for housing development. The Vestry claimed that the pit was Poor's Land which could not be sold. Early in 1888 the Highways Board obtained a court ruling that the land was saleable if the Vestry agreed. The Vestry continued to refuse consent, but supporters of the sale demanded and obtained

a public poll. The vote was 363 for selling, 256 against. The sale accordingly went through, but arguments immediately began over the proceeds. Although the Highways Board accepted they should share them with local interests, the parties could not agree on a formula and went to law again in June 1890. The outcome was that, of about £3,500 raised, the Highways Board and the Poor's Land trustees received less than a third apiece, and the balance went in legal costs.

The third dispute also concerned the railway, as the company offered to double the width of the archway at the Halfway Bridge (then known as Fools Bridge) for a payment of £500. The funds were available, but a local campaign arose to spend the money on reducing the rates rather than hand it to a wealthy railway company. The Vestry accordingly blocked the project but, once again, were overruled in a local poll.

Against this background the first elections for the Walton Urban District Council took place in December 1894. Fifteen members were elected, six each from Walton and Hersham and three from Oatlands. The Walton representatives included Mr McCowan the vicar as

**60**   The Halfway Bridge (Fools Bridge) after the carriageway was widened in the 1890s.

**61**   A more distant view of the bridge, from the Halfway crossroads.

**62** The new Urban District Council at first relied on horse-drawn transport, and one of its vehicles is seen here outside a lodge of Ashley Park. In the 1920s the Council purchased a Ford motor car for staff use, but was criticised for not buying British.

well as Samuel Cresswell, his principal opponent on the School Board, and two prominent local businessmen, George Miskin and Edward Power. Percy Webb, the Vestry clerk, became Clerk to the Council. Although the Council was not legally incorporated until the start of 1895 it held its first meeting a day early, on Saturday 31 December 1894, at the infants school. Its search for permanent premises was very prolonged. Initially the various officers worked from their homes and the Council rented a room in the house of the Surveyor in which to meet. In 1902 a house on the corner of Hersham Road and Kings Road was leased as the council headquarters. An attempt to take over Mount Felix proved unsuccessful, and the Old Manor House was declined as unsuitable. The Council therefore stayed put until Elm

Grove, which had been offered to it in 1908 and 1912 but rejected as too expensive, was finally purchased in 1921.

Walton's designation in 1895 as an Urban District coincided with a surge in local development and urbanisation. A range of attractive shops and stores is recorded in the memoirs of the period which were later collected by the Walton and Weybridge Local History Society. These indicate that Church Street was the principal shopping thoroughfare, with Birkhead's (so named in 1890, and destined to survive for another 80 years) on one side and Blake's drapery and furnishing shop ('more like an emporium' in the words of Gladys Ward) on the other, opposite the church and next to the *Castle* inn. Beyond that the town ended: Miss V.E. Connolly's recollections state firmly

**63** Hersham Road, where the Council established its first permanent office, photographed in 1906.

**64** Church Street, showing the horse-bus, which served the station, and also some early motor vehicles. A view taken in 1906, the year in which railings were placed round the drinking fountain as a protection from vandalism and in which gas lighting, as here, was replaced by electricity.

**65** Another view of Church Street, seen downhill from the church gate with the *Castle* inn on the right.

that 'civilisation ceased with Miskin's' (the timber yard in Terrace Road). Another diarist, Louise Bale, locates the centre of the town at 'Miss Annett's very old china shop, you went down two steps and there was just room to turn round'. That shop faced the end of Church Street (with its back to what is now Hepworth Way). Next door, at the narrow entrance to Bridge Street, stood the *Duke's Head* inn, faced by Bristow's furniture shop on the opposite corner. The short stretch of Bridge Street nearest the town contained an interesting assortment of premises (including on the right Philipson's Library, the Star Brewery and Love's music shop; on the left, beyond the *Duke's Head*, Hilbrand the clockmaker and Stonebanks Shipping Agency) before widening out at its junction with Thames Street.

As regards housing development, the fast growth which had taken place in the 1850s and '60s slowed somewhat in the years that followed: there was only modest change in Walton between the 1871 census and the early 1890s. In that time Churchfield Road and Winchester Villas were developed; Thames Street was also lined with houses, and building began in some of the newer roads outside the

centre such as Bowes Road and Rydens Avenue. But there was no great expansion into open country. The next 20 years were very different. The pattern of streets between the town centre and Sidney Road was completed with the appearance of Highfield Road and Esher Avenue. Towards the Halfway, Kings Road was built (possibly named for the new reign of 1901, when England had a king for the first time in more than 60 years) and Midway and Crossway were laid out as residential roads. North of Terrace Road there was further new building: previously, only Sunbury Lane had led towards the river, but now Annett, Dudley, Russell and Cambridge roads appeared on the map. The Ashley Park land between Stompond Lane and the railway also came on the market for development.

All this activity reflected a growth in the population of Walton parish to almost 10,000 in the 1911 census, which gave 'building and construction' as the occupation of 14 per cent of those in work. It was exceeded only by domestic service (16 per cent); agriculture (6 per cent) came third. However, Walton's largest single employer fell into none of these categories. It was in fact the town's first factory,

**66** Bridge Street early in the 20th century, with Philipson's Library at number 4 (the present Designers) and the Star Brewery beyond.

**67** Bridge Street, showing the ornate lamp-post which stood outside the *George* inn. To its left is the chimney of the *Bear*.

**68**   Winchester Road was known as Winchester Villas when first laid out at the end of the 19th century. However, its present name was in use by the time the Baptist church was built in 1905.

**69**   Esher Avenue looking north, with the spire of the Methodist church in the background. Many sites, including that of St Erconwald's Church, were still to be developed.

**70**  Kings Road, photographed soon after its development at the turn of the 20th century.

**71**  Midway was laid out before the First World War but, as an unadopted road, had long to wait for a reasonable surface. One of the early residents was Dudley Pound, later to become Admiral of the Fleet.

**72** High Street, looking north. On the right is the chemist's shop where Edward, George and Henry Power embarked in the 1880s on the manufacture of dental instruments.

which had been founded in the 1880s when three brothers, Edward, George and Henry Power, combined their profession of dentist with the manufacture of dental equipment. At first they worked from a shed behind their father's chemist shop in High Street, but after lodging their patent for 'an adjustable stool or seat' in 1888 Edward and George Power moved their machinery into a new workshop in Church Walk. (Henry Power appears not to have joined the firm but remained in dental practice.) In the 1890s their instruments and dentures were marketed by a London firm called Claudius Ash & Son, and in 1902 the two businesses merged under the Ash name with Edward Power, by now a Walton councillor, as managing director. The new firm built a three-storey factory in Churchfield Road and by 1914 had a hundred or so employees. A further merger after the war gave 'Power's Works' (as

it was locally known) its long-standing title of The Amalgamated Dental Company.

Houses for Walton residents and a modern factory were not the town's only turn-of-the-century buildings. A new main post office was built at the Halfway. The railway station was enlarged. New places of worship were established and a hospital was founded. Walton's hospital was largely the initiative of Dr George Drabble, who came to the town from South America where his family had lucrative business interests and his father had been mayor of Buenos Aires. In 1894 he set up surgery in Manor Road and four years later married Eva Gough, whose three brothers were founder-members of the Walton Cricket Club which played on the Sassoons' ground in Ashley Park. She is described in one memoir of the time as 'a most exquisite looking woman, very fair, with a lovely complexion and a beautiful figure',

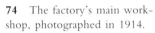

**73** The Dental Factory in Churchfield Road.

**74** The factory's main work-shop, photographed in 1914.

**75**  *Top*. The original Halfway post office was at Ingram's shop, and the crossing was known as Ingram's Corner.

**76**  *Above*. A new purpose-built post office (extreme right) opened in 1908 in Hersham Road.

**77**  *Left*. The Royal Mail. The photograph dates from George V's reign (after 1910) but motor vans have yet to replace horse-drawn vehicles.

**78**   Walton Hospital in Sidney Road. Its foundation stone was laid by the Duchess of Albany in 1904 and it opened a year later. This photograph dates from 1906.

while another recalls flowers being scattered before her at the wedding. In 1900 George Drabble gave up his practice and bought The Grange in Ashley Road. Soon afterwards he and his wife, along with some friends, published a notice saying that 'it was the intention to erect a Cottage Hospital for the more necessitous inhabitants of the Civil Parish of Walton-on-Thames as a Memorial to the Coronation of His Majesty King Edward VII' and appealing for funds to help. The response was such that a six-bedded hospital opened on the corner of Sidney Road and Rodney Road in 1905. Dr Drabble remained the hospital's chairman almost until his death in 1930, and he and his wife made many further gifts for the purchase of land and equipment.

As regards church building, the Methodists had established a chapel in Back Street (which came to be known as Chapel Street, and is now Manor Road) in 1845. But its site attracted the attention of the Walton and Weybridge Gas Company, incorporated in 1869, which wanted to locate its gasworks close to the arrival of coal at Walton Wharf. After long negotiation the company acquired the chapel and its land for

£700. The Methodists spent half of this on a nearby site in Terrace Road, but then needed £3,000 to build there 'a worthy church capable of seating 450 people, together with a schoolroom capable of accommodating the 170 children already in attendance at Sunday school'. This was raised, largely from the local congregation, and the new chapel opened in 1887. By now Walton was no longer part of the Croydon Methodist Circuit: a Chertsey and Walton Circuit had been formed, and in 1905 the Walton minister was made superintendent of it. To mark this, Walton's Methodists bought a house at 10 Hersham Road for their minister to occupy. Most of the money for the purchase came from Emma Steele, youngest daughter of the Joseph Steele who had given the congregation their first building land in 1845.

Across the road from the new Methodist chapel the congregation of St Mary's built their church hall in 1903. The plans for it were drawn up by Arthur Gough, one of the brothers of Eva Drabble. (Mrs Drabble was a strong supporter of the church as well as the hospital: the east window of St Mary's commemorates her parents, Albert and Jane Gough, and she

**79** The Methodists' new chapel in Terrace Road, consecrated in 1887 and here seen across open land.

**80** St Erconwald's. An interior view of the church which served Walton's Roman Catholic community from 1906 until a new, larger building was consecrated in 1937.

also placed a window in the south aisle in memory of her brothers and sister.) Alongside the Anglicans and Methodists, two other churches established themselves in Walton early in the century. A Baptist community was founded in 1903 and one of its members, Joseph Longhurst of West Grove, Hersham, gave land in Winchester Villas (later Road) for an Evangelical Baptist church. It opened in January 1905 with space for about 50 worshippers; a schoolroom and two vestries were added soon after. Mr Longhurst's brother Caleb became the pastor in 1909, but a full-time minister was not appointed until the 1920s. The year after the Baptist church was inaugurated, Roman Catholic worship formally returned to Walton. A local architect, G.B. Carvill, designed a church in Esher Avenue 'in keeping with the other houses on this pretty Estate'. Though superseded by a new larger church in the 1930s, Mr Carvill's building remains as the present church hall. It was dedicated to St Erconwald, the founder of Chertsey Abbey, and the mass celebrated there on Sunday 30 May 1906 was the first in public in Walton since the Reformation.

**81** Station Road (now Station Avenue) with the signpost at the Halfway in the background. An alternative route to the station was offered by a footpath along the line of the present Ashley Park Road.

Along with modern buildings came electric street lighting. The lighting authority was the new Urban District which took over a system of gas lamps in 1895, and sought early economies by not lighting them when there was a full moon. For some years the Council remained wary of investing in electric power in view of the experience of Weybridge, which had pioneered electric lighting in 1891 (one of the earliest towns to do so) but run into such technical problems as to abandon it five years later. A Walton-on-Thames Electric Lighting and Power Company, formed in 1896 and registered at Clark's boathouse, accordingly failed to gain council support and was soon dissolved. But in 1904 the Urban Electric Supply Co. Ltd, which had recently restored Weybridge's electric lighting, approached the Council with a proposal to bring power into Walton from their generating station in Weybridge and light the central area of the town. This was agreed despite some opposition from Weybridge, which had hoped to keep a monopoly of the company's operations. A sub-station was built in Walton and the first 50 street lamps were switched on in 1906. By 1911 there were also 600 private consumers of electricity in Walton.

Another key turn-of-the-century development was the widening of the railway to four tracks and the building of additional platforms at Walton station. Even before this, in the early 1890s, a modern hotel had been built opposite the station and a horse-bus service established between there and the town. It was run by Isaac Stowe, who was a coachman at Ashley Park under the last Sir Henry Fletcher and later acquired a house on the south side of Church Street with stables behind. The two buses he operated were double-deck and open-top, with waterproof aprons fitted to the seats on the top deck for use in rain. Journeys from Church Street were timed to meet the trains, and the conductor rang a handbell to tell intending passengers when the bus was about to depart. From 1906, however, bus travellers faced the risk of an interrupted journey. In that year the Council replaced Walton's 30-year-old fire-fighting equipment by a steam-pump capable of delivering 300 gallons of water a minute and mounted on an engine which it needed two horses to pull. For these they relied on the bus operator. In the words of the local historian, John Stonebanks:

> When the alarm was sounded the driver would draw into the side of the road, unhitch the horses and run them to the fire station in High Street. The bus passengers left at the road side had to make their own way to their destination. The local cabbies might benefit from this situation by their carriages being called for by the stranded passengers.

**82**   Motor vehicles compelled Walton to introduce a 10 m.p.h. speed limit, but they did not have it all their own way. Here are a pony and trap, together with a modern-looking bicycle, outside the *Swan* in 1914.

Both horse-cabs and horse-bus would face competition before long from the internal combustion engine. One very early recollection of a motorised vehicle comes from William Hirons of Crutchfield Lane, who worked for George Miskin and whose tasks included carrying a red flag while walking in front of a traction engine drawing timber from Kingston to Walton. From 1896 red flags were no longer required, and motor traffic increased so rapidly that a 10 m.p.h. speed limit was imposed in central Walton in 1903. Miss V.E. Connolly has left a recollection of seeing Mrs Locke King (of the Weybridge family who owned Brooklands) driving down Walton High Street, though it was not only the motor which left an impression:

> Everyone stood stock still and watched her. I nearly swooned because she was smoking. I knew that women did smoke in strict private, but to smoke in public, in broad daylight, was unheard of. The fact that it was probably the first car I had ever seen passed me by. Over the years it was the cigarette that I remembered.

In 1908 Henry and Ernest Love were given a licence to ply for hire in Walton with a motor car. This put them in competition with John Seaby, the established horse-cab proprietor who also drove for local weddings, and Albert Reynolds who drove a smaller cab or 'fly'. Both horse-drawn and motor taxis remained available until the First World War. An application to run a motorbus service through Walton was received in 1914 from the London General Omnibus Company. The Council turned it down, but almost immediately licensed the Walton Motor Car Co. to operate a route from the river to the station. The Walton fire brigade at first reacted to the loss of the horse-bus by hiring a lorry to tow their engine, but after an embarrassing breakdown invested in a motorised fire engine in 1920.

The last two significant events before the outbreak of war were impressive military funerals at St Mary's. In 1912 the coffin of General Sir Gordon Pritchard, who died at his home in Oatlands Park, was brought to the church on a gun carriage drawn by six horses. Its burial attracted, according to the *Surrey Herald*, 'probably the largest crowd which had ever attended a funeral in Walton Churchyard'. Sir Gordon, born in 1835, was already a soldier at the time of the Indian Mutiny in 1857 and subsequently saw service in China and Africa. In 1913 it was the turn of the navy. Admiral Sir Frederick Bedford served in the Crimean War after enrolling at age 13, and later organised the Nile flotilla which attempted to relieve General Gordon's expedition to the Sudan in 1884. He was appointed an aide-de-camp to Queen Victoria, served as Second Sea Lord,

and was finally governor of Western Australia. From there he retired to a house in Oatlands Chase, whence the naval gun carriage bearing his coffin was hauled into Walton by a company of 36 Petty Officers.

More than 1,000 Walton men served in the First World War. They included the five sons of Joseph Sassoon of Ashley Park, who all saw active service and survived. But among the 117 who lost their lives, and whose names are recorded in St Mary's and on the town's war memorial, are a Burnett (the family who owned The Chestnuts), a Dale (the local butchers and farmers), two Hirons (the hauliers from

**83**   As well as calling Walton's young men to the Forces the war caused hardship at home through food shortages. Here is a queue for potatoes.

**84**   The War Memorial unveiled on a summer's day in 1921. The parasol and some unconventional headgear offered protection from the sun.

Crutchfield Lane who also owned Fishmore Farm), a Seaby (the cab proprietors), two Trinders (who lived at River House) and a Webb (son of the Clerk to the Council). Also there are the two brothers of Gladys Ward, whose recollections tell of the night when the accumulation of bad news was such that a crowd attacked number 5 Bridge Street, the premises of Herman Hilbrand, the clockmaker who was German. According to her account the incident lasted until

> The horse bus drove in from Chertsey with Mr Keswick the Tory M.P. for Walton and extra policemen to control the crowd ... Mr Keswick stood on top of the horse bus by the fountain at the top of Church Street and read the Riot Act.

The armistice came in 1918. Next year, after the signing of the Versailles Treaty, the country devoted the whole of Saturday 19 July to celebrating peace and victory. In Walton there was a parade through the town, bands,

fancy dress, and organised games at Ashley Park. In the evening there was a dance in the church hall, fireworks and a bonfire. Thought was also given to commemorating those who died. The names of the Walton war dead and of the New Zealanders who died in hospital at Mount Felix were recorded at St Mary's, but it was agreed that a permanent outside memorial was needed as well. Dr Drabble chaired the War Memorial Committee which selected a design in Portland stone for a site on the High Street green. On Sunday 10 July 1921, an extraordinarily hot day, the War Memorial was unveiled by Admiral Lord Beatty. In his address he praised the wartime contribution of Walton men and referred to the spirit of Drake and Rodney. Though Walton's Francis Drake (the Cromwellian M.P.) was a different person from the Elizabethan hero, such compliments to local valour were well received by the 3,000 people who came to honour the sacrifice that their families, friends and neighbours had made.

# Seven

# 'Little Hollywood'

A mention of 'the local film studios' would not be taken by present-day citizens of Walton as referring to their town but to Shepperton Studios across the river. Yet from the turn of the century (30 years before Shepperton opened) there was film-making in Walton, and production ceased only in 1961. In the first 25 years of operation, while Walton Studios were run by Cecil Hepworth, their output numbered some 2,000 films, ranging from single-reelers to full-length features and representing about one in six of all the British films of that era. In 1929/30, after Nettlefold Studios took over from Hepworth, Walton was adapted to produce the new talking pictures, and in the 1950s combined the making of films for cinema with productions for television, including the popular *Robin Hood* series.

Film-making began in Walton in 1899 under the trade-name of Hepwix, designating Cecil Hepworth and his cousin Monty Wicks. Hepworth's father had been a science lecturer whose leisure enthusiasm was the magic lantern, and Hepworth grew up fascinated by cameras and photography. His early jobs included the filming of a royal wedding at Marlborough House in 1893 (the participants later became King George V and Queen Mary) and a newsreel of the 1898 Oxford and Cambridge boat race. The following year, aged 25, he set up an independent film-making business with his cousin. Their search for suitable premises brought them to Walton, where they paid £36 a year to rent a house in Hurst Grove, off Bridge Street.

The earliest Hepwix films were one- or two-reelers. (One reel was 50 feet of film, which took about 45 seconds to play; a two-reeler was twice as long.) Their stock-in-trade was short, amusing incidents. There were films called *Comic costume race for cyclists*, *How the Burglar tricked the Bobby* and *Explosion of a motor-car*. Later, in 1905, came *Prehistoric Peeps*, probably the first film to feature dinosaurs (although the

85 Cecil Hepworth (1874-1953), photographed during the First World War. Though continuing to film he was active in the local Volunteers, for whom he provided a rifle range and a drill hall.

**86**    The house in Hurst Grove where Hepwix pictures began.

monsters concerned are clearly actors in skins, who walk like pantomime horses). These films were largely shot with a small camera tracking back and forth. But Hepworth also developed a large heavy camera, nicknamed the 'coffin camera', which held 1,000 feet (15 minutes) of film. This could be mounted on a boat or train, and produced such films as *Thames Panorama*, *Express trains in a cutting* and *Phantom Rides*. It was taken to London for Queen Victoria's funeral where, according to Hepworth's auto-biography, *Came the Dawn*, its noise alerted King Edward VII to the fact that he was being filmed, so that he reined in his horse and posed for photography.

In 1903 and 1905 Hepwix registered two big successes. The first was a 12-minute film of *Alice's Adventures in Wonderland*, based on Tenniel's illustrations and shot in the gardens of Mount Felix. The second was *Rescued by Rover*, a seven-minute drama in which the

Hepworth family (father, mother, baby and dog) all played the equivalent characters in the film. Hepworth did, however, engage two profes-sional actors, the first time he did so, to play the villains of the piece. Their combined fee was £1 1s., from which they had to pay their own fares from London. Even allowing for this expense, *Rover* cost less than £8 to make—but sold almost 400 copies. After this success Hepworth relied increasingly on professional actors and gradually built up a 'stock company' at Walton. But his baby daughter and the family dog, whose name was Blair, did not retire entirely from film-making: they appeared again three years later in *The dog outwits the kidnapper*.

Even when film actors filled his main roles Hepworth still employed local people as his extras. John Stonebanks has recorded how this caused a misunderstanding when a film involving a traffic accident was being made in High Street. According to his account:

> The actor playing the victim having moved out of the field of view of the camera, his place was taken by a dummy in similar attire. Meanwhile a group of onlookers formed around the car and the dummy: these were the 'extras'. But the entry of a local doctor cycling down Churchfield Road had not been envisaged. Unaware of the filming in progress and seeing the group of villagers, he antici-pated the need for his professional services. He dismounted and pushing aside the onlookers knelt down to examine the extent of the victim's injuries. Only then did he realise his mistake and with some embarrassment remounted his bicycle to continue on his rounds.

In November 1907 the Hurst Grove studio was badly damaged by a fire in which one of Hepworth's employees was killed. In *Came the Dawn* Hepworth recalls that friends of the young man, William Lane, formed a choir in his memory which eventually became the nucleus of the local operatic society. In rebuilding the studio the opportunity was taken to introduce more modern equipment. Until then filming was largely outdoors and dependent

**87** A still from Hepworth's film of Queen Victoria's funeral in 1901. Appearing on camera with King Edward VII were Kaiser Wilhelm of Germany (right) and the Duke of Connaught (left).

**88** The Hepworth family dog, who played the lead in *Rescued by Rover*, at the controls of a car with Hepworth's daughter as passenger. Hepworth himself was steering the car from under the bonnet.

on the weather. Chrissie White, who became a leading lady in Hepworth productions, has recorded that her career began as an extra in the school holidays, when summonses from the studio at Walton would say 'Come if fine'.

By 1910 Hepworth had developed the Vivaphone, a combination of camera and gramophone which provided sound to which actors could mime. It was used in some of his films, and equipment for showing these was installed in Walton's Village Hall (on the corner of High Street and Churchfield Road). Hepworth also put his Vivaphone to serious political use. Bonar Law and F.E. Smith, leading Conservatives of the day, came to Walton to record messages promoting their policy of tariff

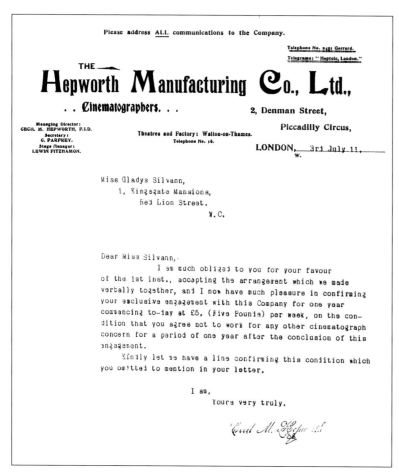

Please address ALL communications to the Company.

Telephone No. 2481 Gerrard.
Telegrams: "Heptolc, London."

THE
**Hepworth Manufacturing Co., Ltd.,**
. . **Cinematographers.** . .

Managing Director:
CECIL M. HEPWORTH, F.I.D.
Secretary:
G. PARPREY.
Stage Manager:
LEWIN FITZHAMON.

Theatres and Factory: Walton-on-Thames.
Telephone No. 16.

2, Denman Street,

Piccadilly Circus,

LONDON, ___3rd July 11,___
W.

Miss Gladys Silvann,
    1, Kingsgate Mansions,
        Red Lion Street.
            W.C.

Dear Miss Silvann,
        I am much obliged to you for your favour
of the 1st inst., accepting the arrangement which we made
verbally together, and I now have much pleasure in confirming
your exclusive engagement with this Company for one year
commencing to-day at £5. (Five Pounds) per week, on the condition that you agree not to work for any other cinematograph
concern for a period of one year after the conclusion of this
engagement.
        Kindly let me have a line confirming this condition which
you omitted to mention in your letter.

        I am,
            Yours very truly,

            Cecil M. Hepworth

**89**  Offer of a film job at Walton, 1911.

reform. Later, in wartime, Hepworth's political connections led to his being invited to film a meeting of the Lloyd George cabinet, but the session was cancelled at the last minute.

In 1911 a permanent acting company was formed at Walton with 22 people under contract. From then on, Hepworth's output was a blend of short amusing films and full-length features of an hour or more. On the lighter side Chrissie White and Alma Taylor took the leads in a series of films about Tilly the Tomboy. More seriously, the company engaged the actor Forbes Robertson to play in a film version of *Hamlet* (building themselves an Elsinore Castle on location at Lulworth Cove in Dorset) and followed this with screen adaptations of *Oliver Twist* and several other Dickens novels. According to Louise Bale of

the *Swan*, 'They did most of the Dickens films in a little alley-way next to the *Manor Pub*. They were tiny Dickens type cottages and the money the occupants got, paid for their winter fuel and rent.' Miss Bale performed as a film extra from time to time, as did her father the pubkeeper, who commanded a handsome 7s. 6d. a day as he resembled a lord. Other occasional players were Pansy Seaby (daughter of the cab proprietor, who lent horses and vehicles to the studio) and the young John Stonebanks, one of a group of schoolboys, paid 2s. 6d. instead of the usual 1s. as they had to wear period costume, who were taken by horse-bus to film in Halliford. During the making of *David Copperfield* in 1914 Reggie Sheffield, who played David as a boy, brought a friend from Teddington to the studio, but Hepworth rated

**90** Forbes Robertson as Hamlet, 1913.

**91** Extras in 18th-century dress during the making of *Barnaby Rudge* in 1915 (accompanied by some local children with a bicycle).

the young man 'an awkward fellow' and did not offer him a job. His name was Noel Coward.

The outbreak of the First World War did not, at first, have a major impact on film-making or film-going. Hepworth's sequence of Dickens films continued in production. Elsewhere in Walton the first purpose-built cinema, the Palace, opened in 1915 (in Church Street, on the site now occupied by the *Regent* public house). The same year the readers of *Picturegoer* magazine, asked to name their 'favourite British film player', put Alma Taylor in first place and Chrissie White in fifth. (Charlie Chaplin came third.) However, the Hepworth management was protective of its stars' privacy. In August

1916 its fans' magazine responded to 'numerous inquiries' that 'we really cannot answer such very intimate questions as to whom they are married, are they divorced, how many children, their private addresses, etc.'.

From 1916 the call-up of men for the forces and other war work began to have a serious affect on film production. At one point Hepworth complained to the Kingston Military Tribunal that he had lost all but six of his 41 male staff, but the tribunal was not sympathetic: 'Picture theatres are an unnecessary luxury', their reply ran, 'and the public will benefit by their closing.' The studio nevertheless remained in business, making a reduced number of feature films and supplementing these

**92**  *Above left.* Alma Taylor, voted the *Picturegoer's* favourite British player in 1915, took the lead in many Hepworth films. She retired in the 1930s but reappeared in a cameo role in *The Pure Hell of St Trinian's* in 1957.

**93**  *Above right.* Chrissie White, another Hepworth star. She married Henry Edwards, who joined the company in 1916, and they formed their own film unit after Hepworth's bankruptcy in 1924.

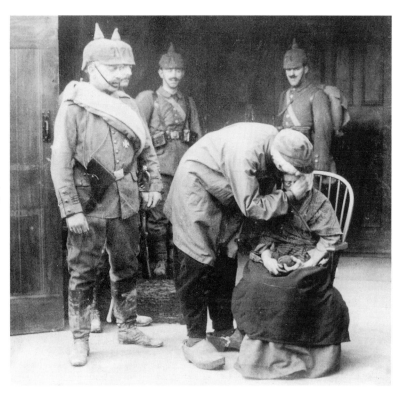

**94** A scene with German soldiers from a wartime Hepworth film.

with propaganda for war bonds and other government initiatives. Hepworth and his company also boosted local morale in 1917 with a garden party for the New Zealanders of Mount Felix, hosted by Alma Taylor and held in the grounds of Ashley Park.

The war ended in 1918, and the studio released only nine films in the following year. But Hepworth then embarked on a big programme of peacetime expansion. He acquired additional land in Oatlands (including part of the Broadwater lake); put in hand the building of a film laboratory and six new studios at Hurst Grove; and, lacking enough electric power for so much extra film-making, arranged to buy the generators from two captured German U-boats and transport them from Liverpool to Walton. Unfortunately he did not have, and could not raise, the capital required for all these ventures. When a prestige production, a two-hour film called *Comin' Thro' the Rye*, took £10,000 to make in 1923 and failed to cover its costs, he admitted failure and went into bank-

ruptcy. Receivers took over the assets of the studios. These included the negatives of Hepworth's films which were sold for industrial use, so that most early Walton films are now lost.

But this was not the end of cinema at Walton or of Hepworth's association with the town. The studios were sold to Archibald Nettlefold, a Birmingham businessman, and resumed production under his name. Hepworth directed one of Nettlefold's early films. One of Hepworth's associates, George Carvill (the architect of St Erconwald's Church), bought the building which had been erected for the electricity generators and turned it into a small theatre named the Playhouse. Dame Ellen Terry laid the foundation stone in September 1925, and it opened three months later. The first Playhouse production was *The Mikado*, performed by the Walton Players (later the Amateur Operatic Society) with Carvill playing Pooh-Bah and Hepworth as musical director.

**95**  Dame Ellen Terry, in Walton to lay the foundation stone of the Playhouse in 1925.

**96**  The Capitol cinema in 1931. Clifford Spain mounted a roof display to publicise *Hell's Angels*, starring Jean Harlow.

Another of Hepworth's early colleagues was Clifford Spain, who had worked for him before the war as actor, cameraman and projectionist before leaving Walton to run cinemas elsewhere. He returned in 1927 as manager of the new Capitol cinema, on the site of the present Screen. When the Capitol was adapted in 1930 to show 'the talkies', Spain issued a special brochure to mark the event: in it Walton is described as 'Little Hollywood'. Besides showing other people's films, Clifford Spain also made and screened his own. These were newsreels of local happenings—galas, sports fixtures, and public events like the coronation celebrations for George VI—and were shown in his cinema alongside feature films. In 1938 Spain left the Capitol to manage Walton's 'super-cinema', the 2,000-seat Regal in New Zealand Avenue. Its grand opening was attended by the Kneller Hall band and Fanfare Trumpeters; as the Regal's organ was

**97** Local celebrations of the 1937 coronation, filmed for a Clifford Spain newsreel.

**98** The Regal cinema under construction in 1937 in the recently opened New Zealand Avenue.

an exact replica of the B.B.C. theatre organ, the maestro of that instrument, Reginald Fort, came to Walton to play at the ceremony.

Meanwhile Nettlefold Studios also made the transition from silent films to sound. Their main output was 'quota films', the British 'second features' which, under the rules of the time, had to make up a proportion of all films shown so as to reduce the dominance of American imports. Their quality was generally modest: a film magazine described Walton production as 'middle-class, mild and conventional'. But business was also good: another trade paper called Nettlefold 'the most consistently busy studio in the country' against competition which, from 1932, included

Shepperton. In 1937 purchase of The Croft, a house in Bridge Street, provided new offices, an extra sound stage and a deep water tank for special effects. But early in the Second World War filming at Walton was suspended. The Vickers factory at Weybridge was bombed in September 1940, and Nettlefold Studios was among the sites taken over to continue its work. Aircraft wings were assembled there.

Film-making resumed in 1946. Nettlefold inherited two hangars from Vickers which could be used as extra stages. They also signed a contract entitling Columbia Pictures to make films at Walton for six months each year. This concession, which ran for three years, brought over a number of American stars, including Rock

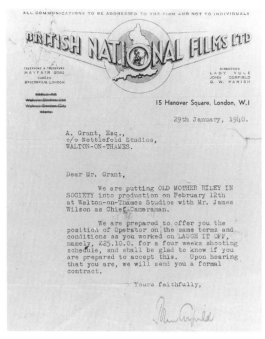

ALL COMMUNICATIONS TO BE ADDRESSED TO THE FIRM AND NOT TO INDIVIDUALS

**BRITISH NATIONAL FILMS LTD**

TELEPHONE & TELEGRAMS                                    DIRECTORS
MAYFAIR 9082                                              LADY YULE
CAREES                                                    JOHN CORFIELD
BRICORFILM, LONDON                                        G. W. PARISH

15 Hanover Square, London, W.1

29th January, 1940.

A. Grant, Esq.,
c/o Nettlefold Studios,
WALTON-ON-THAMES.

Dear Mr. Grant,

      We are putting OLD MOTHER RILEY IN
SOCIETY into production on February 12th
at Walton-on-Thames Studios with Mr. James
Wilson as Chief Cameraman.

      We are prepared to offer you the
position of Operator on the same terms and
conditions as you worked on LAUGH IT OFF,
namely, £25.10.0. for a four weeks shooting
schedule, and shall be glad to know if you
are prepared to accept this.  Upon hearing
that you are, we will send you a formal
contract.

                  Yours faithfully,

**99**   Offer of a film job at Walton, 1940.

**100**   *Come Dance with Me*, an early post-war film with Sidney James (centre) and Hughie Green (right), both to become better-known later.

Hudson, Bette Davis and Zsa Zsa Gabor. Some leading British film actors of the day, such as Margaret Lockwood, Joan Greenwood and Dennis Price, filmed at Walton too. There were two further Dickens films: *Scrooge*, with Alastair Sim, and *Mr Pickwick*, with James Hayter, in which the Old Manor House featured as Dingley Dell.

However, the main post-war development was the arrival in the early 1950s of Hannah Weinstein of Sapphire Films. Mrs Weinstein took a stake in Walton Studios after her left-wing views made it hard for her to obtain work in Hollywood. Her expertise was in producing films for television and she struck a deal with Robin Hood Flour of the U.S.A. who were interested in sponsoring a series about that hero's exploits. Half-hour episodes were made and screened at weekly intervals for about four years. Richard Greene played Robin, and the regular company included Paul Eddington (later famous for *The Good Life* and *Yes, Minister*) as Will Scarlett. Exterior scenes were shot in and around the studio or, where a wilder land-scape was required, on Chobham Common.

Popular success was such that the *Daily Mirror* reported in 1957 that '*Robin Hood* has one of the biggest T.V. audiences in the world. 70 million viewers see it each week in Britain, America and Canada.'

While Sapphire Films produced material for television—which included *The Adventures of Sir Lancelot* and *Sword of Freedom*, as well as *Robin Hood*—cinema films also continued to be made at Walton. *Oscar Wilde*, starring Robert Morley, was filmed there in 1959. But the old-fashioned studios lacked the up-to-date equipment necessary to sustain all this activity and remain competitive. As in Hepworth's day, a modernisation programme was launched but the money to finance it could not be found. The film companies went into liquidation, and the studios closed in March 1961. The local authority bought them for development as Walton's new centre, and more than 60 years of film-making came to an end. The new town lay-out did, however, offer one appropriate reminder of the area's former role: Hurst Grove, where the studios began, now has its entrance into a thoroughfare called Hepworth Way.

**101** Joan Greenwood and Margaret Lockwood in *The White Unicorn*, 1947. Also in the cast was Stewart Rome, an original member of Hepworth's stock company who lodged at the *Swan* for many years.

**102** Dennis Price filming a post-war costume drama.

**103**  Bette Davis at a birthday party in Walton studios while making *Another Man's Poison* in 1951. The film also starred her husband, Gary Merrill (next to her, in a dark tie and waistcoat).

**104**  Richard Greene as *Robin Hood*.

**105**  Barbara Hepworth (Cecil Hepworth's elder daughter, and the baby in his 1905 success *Rescued by Rover*) talking to John Stonebanks in 1974. The occasion was the 75th anniversary of the founding of the studios.

# Eight

# Twentieth–century Walton

'Walton was never the same again', wrote Louise Bale of the period after the First World War. 'People had discovered us. Firms moved out of London with their staff during the war, and afterwards many of the people stayed.' Whether the demand came from London in-comers or from Walton men returning from the Forces, there was certainly a post-war demand for new housing. Walton Council accordingly took advantage of a 1919 law whereby local authorities could draw on government financial help if they provided cheap rented accommodation for 'the working classes'. Their first project was for 200 houses at Selwyn Green (an area described by Gladys Ward as 'all blackberry lanes' and now covered by the St John's estate). The first 50 homes were ready for occupation by 1921 and the rest followed soon after. In 1929 the Council acquired some adjoining land from the owners of Cottimore and developed it as Cromwell Road.

Once the Council began to spend rate-payers' money on subsidised housing its proceedings steadily became more political. Although candidates did not have formal party labels until after the Second World War, two of those who stood in 1920 were sponsored by the local trades council. These 'Labourites' (as the *Surrey Herald* called them) did not do well. A more successful campaign was mounted by Percy Huckins, a gardener at River House, whose election statement proclaimed his 'sympathy with the working classes'. The paper thought he was 'likely to secure considerable

**106** Louise Bale, whose family kept the *Swan* from 1911, seen here with her dog in the early 1920s.

support, especially in the Terrace-road portion of the Parish', and in the event Mr Huckins came within 30 votes of unseating one of the existing councillors. In 1921 he topped the poll, and was still a Walton representative when the joint Walton and Weybridge council was formed in 1933. One of his early campaign issues was the absence of a public park in Walton. The Council responded by opening up the grounds of its new headquarters at Elm Grove and, in 1930, laying out a new recreation ground between Terrace Road and the river.

Municipal housing was only one feature of Walton's development in the 1920s. Another major change was the building of shops on the west side of High Street, where the Ashley Park frontage had been. This offered modern competition to the established stores in Church Street and Bridge Street. Elsewhere in the town centre the cluster of residential roads off Thames Street (Dale, Harvey and Mayo roads) was finally completed. There was further new housing off Terrace Road, and a start to building

in the Walton Park area where Rydens Road meets Ambleside Avenue. Along the Hersham Road, where the grounds of The Chestnuts were sold for development, part of the land was acquired by a Presbyterian congregation which had been hiring the Playhouse for a weekly service for several years. Lord Beaverbrook laid the foundation stone of their new St Andrew's Church in November 1931, and it opened for worship three months later. Another new public building was Rodney House, the maternity home alongside the hospital in Sidney Road. This was a further benefaction of George and Eva Drabble, who also bought a nearby house as nurses' accommodation.

Despite all the development of the 1920s some large Walton houses remained as private homes. Cottimore was occupied by Lady Egmont until 1920 and by the McArthur family until 1934. River House was bought by Archibald Boyd-Carpenter who came to London in 1918 as M.P. for a Yorkshire

**107** Miss Bale wrote that people 'discovered' Walton after the First World War, but the traffic was not all one way. Here is a group from the town setting off to the Derby in 1919.

**108**  High Street in the 1930s, now developed on both sides.

**109**  Miss V.E. Connolly wrote that early in the century 'civilisation ceased with Miskins' (the timber yard, which became Gridley Miskins in 1921). But between the wars development proceeded well beyond that, along a built-up Terrace Road.

**110** St Andrew's Presbyterian Church in Hersham Road, built in 1931-2 as the land around The Chestnuts was opened up for housing and shortly before Oakfield was demolished and redeveloped.

constituency and held office in the Conservative administration of 1922/3. Sir Archibald, as he became in 1926, was out of Parliament during the Labour governments of 1924 and 1929, but secured nomination for the Chertsey division, which included Walton, at the 1931 election. Until his death six years later he was the town's M.P. as well as a leading local resident. Gladys Ward recalls him and his wife Annie as small, good-natured people who were always laughing. (Their son John Boyd-Carpenter later served as M.P. for Kingston; he was joined in Parliament by another Walton man, Harold Watkinson, whose family managed Blake's store in Church Street and who became the Member for Woking. The two men were colleagues in the Macmillan government of the 1950s.)

As Walton grew, so its transport needs increased. Before the First World War the

Council had refused permission for a motor-bus service through the town, but by 1930 the London General Omnibus Company were operating routes 61 and 62 from Kingston to Staines via Walton. The 61 ran through Weybridge and Chertsey, and its Walton–Staines section became green route 461 after London Transport took over the company in 1933; the 62 served Shepperton and Laleham, and London Transport renumbered it 218. Car ownership also grew, and a building which Hepworth Studios had used for scene-painting and construction was converted in the mid-1920s into a garage and petrol station, fronting onto Bridge Street. Now H.W. Motors, it was the first in Walton to instal electric petrol pumps, and after the Second World War its proprietors, John Heath and George Abacassis, made names for themselves by producing, and competing in, the H.W.M. racing car.

Adventurous travel was also promoted by the Stonebanks Shipping Agency, owned by F.G. Stonebanks, father of the historian John. The Agency specialised in arranging emigration passages to Canada and holidays for people with friends or family there. In the early 1930s the elder Mr Stonebanks won a competition by selling 300 tickets for a cruise on the *Olympic* (surviving sister-ship of the *Titanic*) and Cunard rewarded him and his family with a three-day voyage on the ship.

By 1932 the national growth in unemployment had sufficiently affected Walton that 1,600 men were signing on and the Playhouse was in use as a temporary Labour Exchange. Government assistance for new council housing was also suspended. But the country's economic troubles do not seem to have restrained the town's development at all seriously. In 1933 Walton merged with Weybridge in a combined urban district (with 27 councillors: 15 from Walton and 12 from Weybridge): one of the first acts of the new authority was to agree the funding for a through road to take Walton Bridge traffic out of the town centre. It was named New Zealand Avenue in memory of the military hospital at Mount Felix, and the New Zealand High Commissioner attended its formal opening in November 1935. In 1936 the Southern Railway built a new station at Hersham, and the following year rail travellers benefited from the electrification of the line. New housing arose along Ashley Park Avenue and, after the sale of Cottimore and its estate, Stuart Avenue and its adjacent roads were laid out for development. Further homes and roads were also built around Walton Grove, while nearby in Terrace Road there opened the *John o' Gaunt* (later the *Walton*), the town's first new public house for 50 years.

More plans were being laid as the 1930s came to an end. In 1938 the Council acquired a site in New Zealand Avenue for a town hall. They also brought piped water to Fieldcommon as a precursor to regenerating the area, which had become something of a shantytown since

the First World War. Nearby the Metropolitan Water Board began work on a new reservoir off Rydens Road. But all these projects were suspended on the outbreak of war.

Although air-raid shelters were built in Walton, it was at first considered a safe place to which people could be evacuated from London. Five hundred came to the district in 1939 and another 200 the next year. One family which decided to spend the war in Walton were the Koebels, already refugees from Prague. They lived in Stompond Lane, and their daughter

**111** 'Stop Me and Buy One'. In Walton, as elsewhere, Walls ice-cream tricycles were a popular feature of the 1930s. Forty years later Walls established a closer connection with the town by merging with Bird's Eye and sharing their modern headquarters in Station Avenue.

**112** The municipal offices at Elm Grove, floodlit for King George V's Silver Jubilee in 1935.

**113** New Zealand Avenue, photographed in the first winter of the war (1939/40), four years after its opening. The kerb stones were painted black and white for better visibility in the blackout.

Madeleine attended Ingomar School at the top of Ashley Rise. In 1945 they returned to Czechoslovakia, but soon became refugees again from the Communist government there. This time they went to America, where Madeleine married and went into politics. In the 1990s, as Madeleine Albright, she became President Clinton's Secretary of State.

On 24 July 1940 Walton was bombed, and another 50 attacks followed between August and December. More than 1,000 houses in Walton and Weybridge were damaged or destroyed. The raids on Walton, which had no obvious military targets, were probably largely overshoots from London, but the Vickers factory in Weybridge was deliberately attacked on 4 September and 83 people were killed. After this a number of Walton premises, including Nettlefold studios, the dental factory and several garages, were taken over as dispersal sites for the manufacture of aeroplane parts. There were further incendiary attacks on Walton in 1941 and in the spring of 1944, damaging St Mary's Church and burning down

Blake's store on the other side of Church Street. In the early hours of 18 June 1944 one of the first flying bombs came down in Bridge Street, close to Drewitts Court, and several people were killed. Thereafter there were almost continuous alerts from these 'doodlebugs' until the end of August, and additional air-raid shelters were provided in the cellars of Mount Felix, but no more fell on Walton. By way of protection the town had a ring of searchlights and a gun in Ashley Park. Walton people also joined the Dig for Victory campaign in great numbers: more than 2,000 allotments were allocated, and the Terrace Road recreation ground was ploughed up for more. Regular War Savings weeks were also held. Much of the money raised was devoted to the equipment and maintenance of the warship HMS *Celandine*, a corvette which Walton and Weybridge 'adopted' in 1942.

Just over 100 service personnel from Walton lost their lives in the Second World War. Among them was Squadron Leader Eric Moxey, killed while trying to defuse an unexploded bomb at Biggin Hill airfield in August 1940 and posthumously awarded the George Cross. Later Moxey's son Nigel was killed in North Africa, as was Hugh Crichton-Melville, whose father was vicar of St Mary's from 1944. Walton also suffered 26 civilian casualties, nine of them in the bombing of Vickers. Peace came in 1945 and was celebrated with street parties and parades. The Council marked victory by applying for a coat of arms for the district, which was granted in March 1946. Its design featured the Thames; the Latin motto *Dum defluat amnis* translates as 'till the river runs dry'.

Though some things rapidly returned to normal (street lighting was switched on, and

**114**   V.E. (Victory in Europe) Day, 1945. A street party in Rydens Avenue.

church bells were allowed again), full recovery from the physical and economic effects of war took a long time. The main priority was housing. The Council undertook a large building programme, and although it began slowly—with fewer than 100 new homes by the end of 1947—the 1,000th post-war council house was occupied in 1954. Most of Walton's development was off Cottimore Lane and around Vicarage Fields. The need to retain open spaces for the town to counterbalance the new building was recognised by the Council's purchase of the Cottimore lake area, which became the George Froude Park; of River House, whose grounds became a riverside public garden; and of 20 acres of Cowey Sale.

In 1950 Walton's outlying estates were allocated a new bus service, the 264, which came into town from Hersham Green by way of Ambleside Avenue and Cromwell Road. This completed a pattern of services which lasted a further 20 years. Three red London Transport routes ran to Kingston: the 264 by way of Sunbury and Hampton, the 218 through Esher, and the double-decker 131 through Molesey. Three green routes, also double-deck until 1970, ran to Weybridge and beyond: the 461 to Staines; the 461A to Botley's Park, Chertsey, where a small local hospital was being developed into the modern St Peter's; and the 463 to Guildford. Their Walton terminus was at the Odeon, formerly the Capitol cinema and now the Screen, and the triangle of streets round which the buses turned was made one-way in 1964. Two long-distance Green Line routes, 716 and 716A, served the town too, starting in Hertfordshire, passing through London, and terminating at Chertsey Bridge and Woking respectively. Finally, the service from the bridge to the station, begun by the Walton Motor Car Co. in 1914, ran until 1970, when its 20-year-old vehicle failed the M.o.T. test and had to be withdrawn.

The years until 1960 were generally a quiet time for Walton, but at least one local personality made headlines. Julie Andrews was

**115** Coat of arms of Walton and Weybridge, granted in 1946. (Prior to that, Walton's emblem was a swan.) On the arms the wavy line represents the Thames, the roses refer to the area's Tudor connections—notably Oatlands Palace—and the eagle to Roman legions crossing the river.

born in the Rodney House maternity home in 1935. Her family spent the war in Kent before returning to the Old Meuse, a house in West Grove with a large studio. Here Ted and Barbara Andrews not only prepared their own stage and radio performances but saw to it that Julie's singing and acting talents were nurtured and developed. Another contributor to her success was Barbara Andrews' sister, Joan Morris, a leading local dance teacher for many years. Julie Andrews made her first West End appearance at the London Hippodrome at the age of 12. Among those who saw her there was Tony Walton, a local boy of her own age, who was taken to London for a birthday treat. He recognised her on the train home, got in touch

**116**   High Street in 1947.

**117**   Post-war Church Street (still empty of traffic).

**118**   An attraction for children was the Pet Shop in New Zealand Avenue.

the following day, became a close friend, and eventually developed his own theatrical career as a stage designer.

In her teens Julie toured London and the provinces in variety, combining her own singing spot with supporting roles for other artists. At 19 she played in pantomime at the London Palladium, after which she received an offer of the lead role in the Broadway production of *The Boy Friend*. She accepted with some misgivings, and her family saw her off to New York from a half-built Heathrow. But her success was such that she was next invited to

create the role of Eliza Doolittle in *My Fair Lady*, and returned in it in 1958 for the London production at Drury Lane. The following year she and Tony Walton were married at St Mary's, Oatlands. Their daughter Emma was born in London in 1962, before they left to film *Mary Poppins* (she as star, he as designer) and pursue their careers in America.

Despite new housing estates and its steady improvement as a shopping centre, Walton remained essentially unchanged between the opening of New Zealand Avenue in 1935 and the early 1960s. Then redevelopment began

**119** In Bridge Street, Walton children could enjoy the Toy Shop (seen here, next to the *George* inn) and the Rainbow Book Shop.

**120** A bus service from Kingston to Staines by way of Esher, Walton and Shepperton began after the First World War. From 1933 until its privatisation some 50 years later it was run by London Transport as route 218. This bus is approaching the stop at the Halfway post office from which, in the mid–1970s, the service was diverted to call at Walton station.

121   Julie Andrews photographed at the Waltons' house, Nethercliffe in Ashley Road.

122   Tony Walton at his boarding school, Radley College. Tony's father was Lance Walton, a leading orthopaedic surgeon and authority on the treatment of polio. The family lived briefly in Midway before moving to Ashley Road in 1934.

again and a surge of new building transformed the town. This was partly because funds were now available for long-planned projects. But another factor was a change in the law which allowed Poor's Land, if not required for its primary purpose of allotment holdings, to be sold off at market value. Such sales brought in a very large income for Walton Charities as prime land was released for development. Among the first to become available was a six-acre site between the Halfway Green and the railway station. In 1959 the Council bid £28,000 for it as the location for an indoor swimming pool—but changed their minds and withdrew the offer. The trustees of the land, whose previous income from it had been about £8 a year, sold instead to Bird's Eye Frozen Food Company for more than £100,000. Bird's Eye commissioned an office building from Sir John Burnet, Tait and Partners, with a brief that it should still look modern in 20 years' time. The outcome was a long, low structure with an ornamental pond in front and two courtyards at the rear, further distinguished by a pool for alligators in the lobby!

**123**  Birkheads in 1910.

**124**  Birkheads in 1961. Miss Connolly wrote that the right-hand side of Church Street 'was very little changed ... till the supermarkets came'. Here are two photographs of its leading store, taken 50 years apart.

**125** The interior of the swimming pool, designed by Ove Arup and praised by Pevsner and Nairn as Walton's best modern building.

The next major construction was the new reservoir, with capacity for about 4½ billion gallons of water, on former farmland between Rydens and Fieldcommon. The Queen opened it in March 1962 as the Queen Elizabeth II Reservoir. The official ceremony included tea in a specially built pavilion with music from the band of the Irish Guards, and among the guests was Dr Charles Hill, Minister of Housing and Local Government. Dr Hill was something of a local hero at the time, as he had just rejected the recommendation of a Royal Commission on London Government to take Walton and Weybridge Urban District (and neighbouring Esher) out of Surrey to become part of the Borough of Kingston, under the authority of a new Greater London Council.

After failing to secure a site at the Halfway for a swimming pool, the Council made use instead of a corner of the Elm Grove recreation ground. A design was commissioned from Ove Arup and Partners, and the building, approached by a new road called Kings Close, was completed in 1965. Six years later it was singled out for praise in Pevsner and Nairn's survey of Surrey buildings as 'the most satisfactory recent building in Walton (and one of the best in Surrey)'. The authors describe it as having an 'extraordinarily light and airy' effect, both from its good design and because 'the west wall is all of glass, looking out over the park'.

The same year as the swimming pool opened Walton acquired its brand-new town centre, a development made possible by the Council's purchase of the Nettlefold studio site in 1961. The new Hepworth Way was built as an extension to Church Street, linking up with Bridge Street by the Playhouse. This offered a faster traffic route from the shopping centre to the bridge, ending the serious bottleneck at the southern end of Bridge Street and allowing it to become one-way. On the right of Hepworth Way three ten-storey blocks of flats were erected and named Wellington Close. On its left appeared the new Walton Centre, served by a multi-storey car park and grouped around Campbell and Booker's (now Beale's) department store, with a frontage on New Zealand

**126**   Walton's new central crossroads, showing the junction of Church Street and High Street with Hepworth Way.

Avenue. The Centre's architects were R. Seifert and Partners, who designed London's Centre Point at about the same time.

The remodelling of Walton was completed by the building of a town hall on the land which the Council had long earmarked for it in New Zealand Avenue. A firm of architects, Sir John Browne, Henson and Partners, was appointed in the 1950s to design a building which would offer the Council and its officers an adequate replacement for their cramped surroundings at Elm Grove. The result was a three-storey, three-winged office with a garden frontage, on which work began in 1963.

The town hall was formally opened by Princess Margaret in October 1966. Among the guests at the ceremony was a group of visitors from Rueil-Malmaison on the western outskirts of Paris, who were the first to come to Walton under the new twinning arrangement. They were led by M. Pourtout who had been mayor of the French town since the 1930s and who now found himself unexpectedly presented to British royalty. Twinning was the initiative of Paul Vanson, leader of the Labour group on Walton and Weybridge council, whose uncle was Rueil-Malmaison's deputy mayor. At Easter 1966, six months before the town hall ceremony,

a coachload of local people made the inaugural trip to France: they included rugby and soccer teams who played matches against the Rueil Athletic Club, which Councillor Vanson's father had founded in 1910. A twinning guild was soon set up to oversee these alternating visits, which were inherited by the Borough of Elmbridge when it absorbed Walton and Weybridge in 1974 and continue to this day.

Paul Vanson, who came to England in 1933 and to Walton in 1939, became a councillor in 1952, one of two Labour members facing 25 Conservatives. Over the next ten years, however, Labour and Liberal representation in Walton and Weybridge increased to the point where, for just one year, their combined support reached 14 to the Conservatives' 13. This allowed Jack Shaw, who sat for Labour in Walton North, to become the only member of a minority party to chair the Council. But the keenness of local party politics did not reflect any serious disagreement over the priority which the Council gave to house-building. In 1964 a private Bill gave the necessary power to convert three-quarters of the Terrace Road recreation ground into the land for the new Thamesmead estate. There was also progress with housing development at

Fieldcommon. In 1964 proper sewerage was installed and permission given for 100 private homes; next year the Council bought the land necessary to build a further 125 houses, a public hall and some shops. Fieldcommon was thus gradually drawn into the Walton community, though a bus service through the estate had to await the mid-1970s.

In September 1968 a sudden, unexpected disruption hit the town. On the weekend of the 14th and 15th, after several weeks of wet weather, more than three inches of rain fell in 24 hours. Early on Monday 16th the Mole burst its banks at Esher Road, Hersham. Floodwater flowed through the Longmore estate and ran three feet deep through the railway bridge at Hersham Station. From there a stream along Molesey Road flooded Fieldcommon; another down Walton Park ('like a river' according to one eye-witness) left Rydens Road 'like some large lake' and reached the Cottimore area in mid-afternoon. By midnight Garden Road and The Grove were flooded and the water had reached Sunbury Lane, Cambridge Road and adjoining streets on its way to the Thames. As people had to leave their homes the town hall, the Playhouse and the town's church halls were opened to provide emergency food and shelter.

Recollections of the flood (now held at the Elmbridge museum) include a motorist told by the police that the only way into Fieldcommon was to swim: most residents had been evacuated by lorry. A householder in Rydens Road recalls one young neighbour canoeing to Molesey to discover what was happening. Someone living safely on the seventh floor of Vicarage Fields saw 'two men and a dog in a punt coming down Second Avenue'. A resident of First Avenue who was marooned for most of the week (the street was not pumped out until Saturday 21st) wrote of

> dirty brown and oily water all around the house and along the road in which fish that had been swept out of ponds could be seen swimming ... During the day a lorry would turn up to take people to dry land to go to work or shopping ... On one occasion a boat was rowed up the road, tied up to our gate post and took orders for tea, sugar, cigarettes etc., rowed back to the local shop, then back with the goods. We lived and ate upstairs during this time but had to carry the cat out to some dry ground twice a day.

Though the Council were criticised for late warnings of the Mole (and the Wey) reaching dangerous levels, there was general praise for the help they offered in cleaning up and drying out. The cost to ratepayers of the flood was about £30,000. It proved almost the last big challenge faced by Walton and Weybridge

**127** Hepworth Way, photographed from the multi-storey car park with Wellington Close opposite and Mount Felix in the background. The bus is a 131, its route originally from Walton to Kingston but extended to Wimbledon in 1962 when trolleybuses were withdrawn.

**128** The Centre around 1974, showing the kiosk and sculpture alongside Grant Warden, the department store. Grant Warden opened as Campbell and Booker and was subsequently bought by Beale's.

**129** The new town hall. Its garden fronted onto New Zealand Avenue.

Council before a government white paper called for fewer, larger local authorities, and negotiations began on joining with Esher in a new borough. Agreement was reached on a combined authority of 60 councillors (as against the 27 who had run Walton and Weybridge since 1933) with its headquarters, for the time being, at Walton town hall; a larger civic centre was later built in Esher. As for its name, a choice emerged between Claremont (from the former royal residence in Esher) and Elmbridge, the administrative name for the area in Saxon times. Elmbridge prevailed. Meanwhile the last major initiative taken by Walton and Weybridge Council was the 1971 decision to build a sports complex by the river. Work on this began two years later and was still in hand when the merger with Esher took place in 1974. On completion it was named the Elmbridge Leisure Centre, the first flagship project of the new authority.

The extensive redevelopment of Walton in the 1960s for new public buildings and private housing had a cost in the loss of older properties. Pevsner and Nairn's 1971 description of the town mentions the disappearance of 'expensive houses of *c*.1900' and their replacement by 'flats and terrace houses'. These changes caused some local disquiet, especially as interest in the town's heritage was growing: Walton and Weybridge Local History Society dates from 1964. Two developments of the early 1970s led to actual protest. First was the proposal to replace Birkhead's, which had stood in Church Street as long as anyone could remember, by a supermarket. A campaign to save the store was unsuccessful. It was demolished along with Snell's, the drapers next door, and Safeway took their place. The second controversial project was the building of flats at Hillrise, which many feared would spoil the view of the Thames and diminish public access to the river bank. Again, attempts to halt the development did not succeed. But a public meeting, called in November 1975 to protest against the erosion of Walton's heritage, attracted 250 people. From it emerged the Walton Society, dedicated to maintain the town's character and to give citizens a voice where this was threatened. The society thrived, contesting (and winning) its first Council seat within five years and carving out a significant role in the life of the town.

**130** Princess Margaret leaving the town hall with Neil Osborne, chairman of Walton and Weybridge Council, after formally declaring it open on Wednesday 19 October 1966.

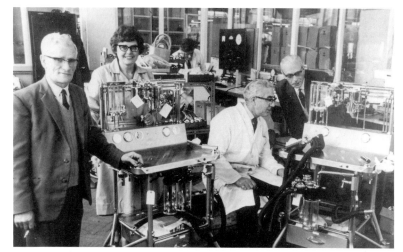

**131** A Walton institution unaffected by the town's redevelopment was the Dental Factory, here seen in 1967. It remained a leading local employer until its closure in 1981.

**132** Florence Road in September 1968. The rower is Frank Wheals, of the Clerk's department of the Council.

**133** Ambleside Avenue in flood.

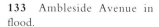

**134** Walton town hall served the new Elmbridge authority until the Council decided (by a chairman's casting vote) to move all its administration to Esher. In 1993 the town hall was demolished and its site sold commercially, to become a Homebase superstore.

**135** The *Castle* in Church Street was a casualty of the town's redevelopment, closing in 1972.

**136** Church Street, showing the empty Birkhead's site. This was photographed during a Mission to Walton by all the local churches in 1974; at the head of the procession is Martin Hussey, carrying the cross.

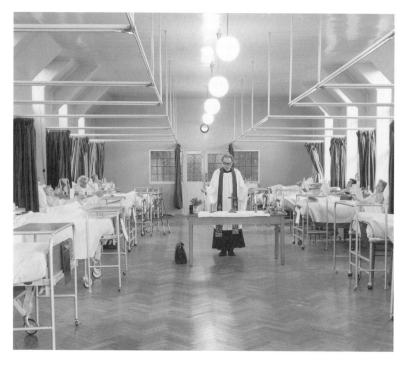

**137** Walton in the 1970s. A communion service at the hospital taken by the Rev. Tony Carter (vicar 1969-79).

*Nine*

# School and Play

In 1634 Francis Drake, of the family who lived at Walton Grove, made a will under which 'ten pounds a yeare' was left 'for the teaching of eighteen poore schollars in the Schoolehouse that I have built upon the Mannor of Walton twelve of Walton and six of Eshere'. A later 17th-century document refers to a road 'leading from the town to the school house and reaching to Field Common', but that is all that is known of Drake's school. By 1725, according to a report from the vicar of Walton to his bishop, there was no endowed school in the parish. In 1788, however, his successor listed four schools, supported by voluntary subscriptions, parental fees or charity, attended by about 70 children in the week and 100 on Sundays.

Early in the 19th century associations were founded for the promotion of National (Church of England) and British (nonconformist) Schools, and in February 1812 the Bishop of Winchester asked parishes in his diocese to establish National Schools. In April the response of the Walton Vestry was to accept the principle but lament the absence of resources to carry it through, but by October they

> Resolved unanimously that with thanks and gratitude we accept his Royal Highness the Duke of Yorks gracious intention of Patronising and assisting in the Establishment of a School for the Education of the Infant Poor of the parishes of Walton and Weybridge in the Knowledge of the Bible etc.

Among the nobility and gentry who joined the duke in this initiative were Lord Tankerville of Felix Mount, Sir Henry Fletcher of Ashley Park and Edward Peppin of Walton Lodge.

The exact date when the school opened is not known, but church records of 1814/15 refer to Job Elphick and to Joseph Crutchfield, the Vestry clerk, as 'school masters'. Elphick's name is also linked to a property which was conveyed in 1827 for use as a school, and which was almost certainly a forerunner of the building (next to the *Plough* inn) which housed the infants school until 1931 and later became the town library. By 1846 the minutes of the National Society indicate that in Walton there was an infants' section with about 70 pupils and a 'mixed school' for 120, with a further 25 children attending in the evening. They were taught by a master and two mistresses. The 1851 census names the women teachers as Sarah Elphick, daughter of Job, and Sarah Bartlett, who continued to teach Walton's infants until 1885; the schoolmaster was George Monk. It also indicates that they used not only the building given in 1827 but also a part of the old workhouse (now the Grange).

Charles Lushington became vicar of Walton in 1851 and took the initiative in planning a new school. Within a year he contacted the Education Committee of the Privy Council (who could grant up to half the cost, provided the rest was met locally) and set out for them the inadequacies of the old workhouse building. However he did not carry all his parishioners with him. A group headed by 'the Rev. Churchwarden' (probably William North) argued that the National School was

**138**  The *Plough* inn and the infants school (right) seen from Ashley Road. The school building later became Walton's public library.

efficiently run and that criticism of it represented an unjustified attack on the schoolmaster. They also took issue with Mr Lushington's inclusion of the nonconformist community in his discussions and his wish to found a school 'to include all Religious Denominations'. After two public meetings the vicar and his supporters prevailed. In 1857 they notified the Education Committee of their intention to build 'a School for 100 boys and 80 girls with houses for the Master and Mistress'. Negotiations were already in hand for the site on which Ashley School now stands, and Walton-on-Thames Parochial School opened there on 1 July 1858. Including the teachers' accommodation it cost around £1,250, of which the promoters raised £722 and the Education Committee met the balance. The new school's management committee was chaired by Charles Lushington, and among its eight members were two leading local Methodists, Joseph Blake and Joseph Steele.

The Education Act 1870 provided for school boards to oversee the education of children aged from five to thirteen. A Walton Board was first elected in 1878 and took over the Parochial School and the infants school (both now renamed Board Schools) in January 1879. It was chaired by the Rev. Thomas McCowan, Lushington's successor as Walton's vicar, and caused a storm in 1882 by excluding the press from its meetings; according to one member, coverage in the *West Surrey Times* resembled 'a sheet of *Punch*'. A protest meeting in Hersham did not persuade the board to change their minds, but members fared badly when they faced re-election in 1884. While Mr McCowan was returned along with two of his supporters, the other six places were won by a group calling themselves 'economists' (from their wish to economise on school expenditure). The new board re-admitted the press and dismissed the serving clerk, appointing Percy

Webb, who was also the Vestry clerk, in his place. But they soon ran into fresh controversy. Samuel Cresswell was their attendance officer, appointed in 1879 in an attempt to dissuade local parents from keeping their children at home to help with farm work. In 1886 the board dismissed him for claiming publicly that lunchtime detentions imposed by a particular teacher were a factor in poor attendance. At the following year's elections to the board most of the 'economists' did not stand, but Cresswell did. He topped the poll, and became the new vice-chairman. After the next triennial election in 1890 he became chairman of a board described in the press as 'radical'.

One of the new board's aims was to adopt the Mimpriss system of religious education, which was devised for nonconformist churches, in place of the Winchester diocesan syllabus. But although they had general control of local education there were still trustees of individual schools, and the trustees opposed the change. Further, as they had control of school premises until 10 a.m. on teaching days, they asked the teachers to conduct religious education before that time. The board overruled them by setting the lesson at midday, and the trustees reluctantly gave way. But when the board came up for election again in 1893 only Cresswell himself and one other radical were returned: a 'church party' headed by Mr McCowan and including the vicars of Hersham and Oatlands took control. Mimpriss teaching was ended, and religious instruction was tactfully put back to the time which the trustees preferred.

In 1902 state education became a county responsibility, which it has remained since. The Walton Board (to which one woman member, Sarah Hawes, had been elected in 1896) was wound up. The Surrey authorities found a number of problems in the Walton schools. First, the buildings were badly run-down. The 'mixed' school for older children lacked proper sanitation, and the gas lighting was adequate in only two of its eight classrooms. Second, epidemics caused frequent school closures. Third, help was needed for some local families: records from 1907 state that 'much distress is prevalent among the poorer boys, many coming to school in a ragged condition and practically bootless', and the following year 'a few pairs of boots have been bought for some of the poorer boys whose fathers have no work'. Finally, there was serious overcrowding. In the infants school there were 165 pupils (and three teachers) in 1901, and 'half the children in the second class have to sit on the floor'. There were also instances of children having to remain in infants classes beyond the age of eight as there was no room for them in the upper school.

**139** A class at the infants school, around 1890.

**140**   A classroom in the infants school, 1909/10.

The county's response to overcrowding was to open two new schools. The first was an additional infants school on the site of the present Grovelands, serving the area east of Russell Road. Officially called East Walton, it was always known as the 'tin school' from its corrugated iron structure. It opened in 1908 with 116 children and three teachers. In 1912 a fourth classroom was added, and two years later pupil numbers were up to 200 because of the continuing absence of senior school places to which children could transfer. In 1915 the county addressed that problem by opening a second new school for the town, the Central School in Mayfield Road for children between 11 and 15. Over 400 pupils were enrolled, with a head and eight qualified teachers.

At first the new places for older children brought pupil numbers under control. In the early 1920s there were fewer than 100 infants on roll in either the Walton school or the tin school. But as the town expanded the numbers grew once more. The county's answer in 1931 was to close both schools and open a new one in Ambleside Avenue (then known as Cromwell Road school, and later as Ambleside or Swansmere). The infants school building in Walton became the town library. But the tin school had to re-open after less than two years, and by 1934 was again catering for almost 200 children. In 1938 the county eased the pressure by making further provision for the over-11s, as the Central School (Mayfield) became a girls school, and a Central Boys Council School opened beside the infants school in Ambleside Avenue.

There was never a grammar school in Walton, although Surrey offered scholarships (free from 1907, but means-tested from 1932) to 11-year-olds who won grammar school places elsewhere in the county. The first pupil from the Board school in Ashley Road to obtain entry to Tiffins School in Kingston did so in 1898, and by the 1930s the school was celebrating the winning of several county scholarships each year. The Education Act 1944 formalised the arrangements for selection, so that any Walton child who passed the '11-plus' examination was offered a place at a Surrey grammar school. Others received a 'secondary modern' education at Mayfield or Ambleside. However, from the 1950s there was limited local provision for 11-plus successes as a new school opened at Rydens with a 'grammar stream'.

Criticism gradually grew of a system whereby academic failure at the age of 11 debarred most children from sixth-form and university education. In 1964 the incoming Labour government required local authorities to draw up plans for all-ability schools. Surrey tabled a scheme for Walton based on the ages of transfer (traditionally seven or eight from infant to junior school, and 11 to secondary school) rising to nine and 13. All pupils over

13 would attend Rydens; Mayfield and Ambleside would become Middle Schools for the age-group below; and children up to nine would be in primary school at Ashley Road, Ambleside or Grovelands (which had replaced the tin school in 1960). This received government approval and was implemented in September 1969. Mayfield and Ambleside both ceased to be single-sex and began to cater for a new, lower age range. At Rydens, which took in all the pupils from those schools who were 13 or over, numbers rose overnight from 700 to 1,200.

Within a year, however, these arrangements were under review. There were several reasons. First, the growing number of school-age children meant that Rydens would have to cater before long for another 200 pupils, and neither new buildings nor temporary classrooms were available for this. Second, there was no prospect of alternative school places in Walton when

**141** Prefects at the Central School in Mayfield Road, 1926. Mayfield became an all-girls school 12 years later.

**142** Danesfield School at its original site in Hersham Road, close to the Halfway bridge. The school closed briefly in 1939 and reopened in Rydens Avenue. The building shown here stood until 1955.

the ageing Mayfield buildings were taken out of commission. Third, when the Conservatives regained power nationally in 1970, a lobby led by Walton's county councillor, Irene Habershon, began to press for the whole strategy to be rethought and selection retained. After fierce debate the County Council opted in 1972 for a non-selective scheme covering Walton and Weybridge together, with secondary education beginning at 12 and the pressure on Walton relieved by the expansion of Heathside and other Weybridge schools. However, the Secretary of State for Education, Margaret Thatcher, declined to approve the plan, as it contained no right for local parents to send their children to selective schools outside the locality by entering them for the 11-plus. It took effect only after a further change of government, being accepted in 1975 by Reg Prentice, the Labour education minister who later crossed the floor and served in Mrs Thatcher's administration.

A number of private schools flourished in Walton alongside those maintained by the county. In 1927 two sisters, Mrs Evans and Mrs James, founded Westward Preparatory School in Hersham Road which still caters there for small boys and girls. Danesfield School, which has similarly survived to the present, began as a girls school at the Halfway and closed temporarily in 1939. After negotiations for new premises, it reopened the following year as a junior school (for girls and boys) under two former teachers, Miss Quartermain and Miss Kaye, and before long moved to its present location in Rydens Avenue. However, during

the year of closure another teacher, Miss Connolly, secured a room in which senior girls who were preparing for examinations could continue their studies. Her initiative developed into Sarum School, which she headed until her retirement in 1965. Sarum eventually took 250 pupils; its main premises were in Oatlands Chase, while a house in Ashley Road accommodated staff and a few boarders. Miss Connolly claimed that it had a democratic ethos in which 'the conduct of affairs was in the hand of the Head Girl and the VIth Form'. Another school for girls (and boys up to eight) was Ingomar, located where Chilton Court now stands and headed by Miss Dunham and Miss Laity, while the local independent boys school was St Martin's in Rydens Road, which also provided boarding places.

The three girls schools, Danesfield, Sarum and Ingomar, not only offered their pupils the usual lessons and sport but catered for their leisure by running girl guide companies. This contributed towards Walton's emergence as a centre for guiding. A company linked to St Mary's Church was founded as early as 1910 by Alice Bussell, the vicar's daughter, and Edith Anderson, a Sunday school teacher, and was registered as the 1st Walton in 1921. Further companies were sponsored by the Methodist, Presbyterian and Roman Catholic churches; together with a second company at St Mary's, brownies at St John's and the guides at the three schools, a post-war peak was reached of nine Walton companies. Walton's sea scouts, with their headquarters in Felix Road, also began before the First World War. But there

**143**   St Mary's brownies photographed in the vicarage garden, 1922.

**144**   In the early 1920s St Mary's also had a flourishing Church Lads' Brigade. Photographed with them is the Rev. W. Kemp Bussell, Walton's vicar 1901-31.

was no mainstream boy scout movement in the town until much later, possibly because scouting was available in Weybridge from 1908 and in Hersham soon after. A Walton troop based at St Mary's began in 1933. Scouting then developed as the guides had done, with the launch of troops associated with the other churches; those at the Methodist church were air scouts. By the 1950s scouting was popular enough to warrant a large new hut in Cottimore Lane, enabling many Walton scouts to enjoy purpose-built facilities instead of meeting in church or school halls.

As well as the uniformed organisations, a number of youth clubs catered for young people in Walton; most were linked to churches, but the County ran one at its depot in Crutchfield Lane. In 1958 came an attraction of a new kind. Two years earlier Deniz Corday, who lived in Bermuda, filmed there with a company from Shepperton Studios and returned with them to England. But he failed to obtain the equity card (that is, membership of the actors' trade union) which would have enabled him to remain in films. Instead he took a job at Birkhead's in Walton, selling records; while there he developed the idea of playing records to which a live audience could dance. He hired the Playhouse for this purpose on Saturday nights, and the Walton Hop began. It was probably the country's first regular disco. It was also an immediate success, with queues for entry and the doors often closing soon after the music had started. Before long, groups came to perform, so that records were interspersed with live music: among those who played at Walton were the Moody Blues and the Bay City Rollers. A feature of the Hop was that performers would mime to well-known records, and a local group led by Jimmy Pursey began their career there miming Bay City Rollers numbers. From this they started to play music of their own as Sham 69, and went on to national success with two hit singles in the top ten in 1978 and a third, *Hersham Boys*, in 1979.

As well as housing the Hop, the Play-house remained the home of local amateur drama. It opened in 1925 for the first produc-tion of the Walton and Weybridge Amateur Operatic Society, which has continued to stage one or two shows a year. At first the society's output was mainly Gilbert and Sullivan operas, but it abandoned these between 1933 and 1939 in favour of musicals of other kinds, such as *The Beggar's Opera* in 1936. After a break for the war years a pattern was established (and has remained largely unchanged) of alternating Gilbert and Sullivan with operas from different traditions such as *Lilac Time* (in 1960), *La Belle Hélène* (1969) and *Carousel* (1976). Meanwhile, from 1936 a dramatic society called Coventure also performed at the Playhouse. A third group was formed after the war, drawing many of its members from the Weybridge Rowing Club. This was the Desborough Players, whose first production in 1947 was the comedy *Quiet Weekend* but who soon became better known for their annual pantomime. The first of these was *Little Boy Blue* in January 1954, and they have continued each winter.

Walton also had much to offer sports enthusiasts. In 1898 Joseph Sassoon made his ground in Ashley Park available to a Walton Cricket Club and served as its president until 1914. The club closed in wartime, and then faced the loss of its pitch when the Ashley Park estate was sold. It revived by merging with the Elm Grove Cricket Club, set up in 1928 for employees of the local council. The Council helped persuade the developers of Ashley Park to restore the cricket ground and rent it back to the club. The link between the local authority and Walton cricket was underlined when George Froude, the team wicket-keeper, served in 1930 both as club vice-captain and chairman of the Council.

The club's president from 1930 was M.R. Jardine, a Middlesex cricketer before the First World War and father of Douglas Jardine, the Surrey captain who led England in 1932/3 on the controversial 'bodyline' tour of Australia. Mr Jardine and his wife Alison, who is

**145**  Walton Hop—the stage.

**146**  Walton Hop—the dance
floor. The Hop began in 1958
and continued until 1990.

**147**   *Trial by Jury* with Henry Hitch as the Learned Judge and Ettie Perry as the Plaintiff.

**148**   *HMS Pinafore* with John Roake as Captain Corcoran and Charles Ryman as Sir Joseph Porter. The Walton and Weybridge Amateur Operatic Society staged these two Gilbert and Sullivan operas at the Playhouse, 26–30 May 1959.

remembered in a plaque in St Mary's Church, lived in Ashley Road. Under his presidency, which lasted until 1947, the club established a strong local team and successfully survived the loss of its ground (to a searchlight battery) during the Second World War. In 1950 George Froude, his playing days now over, became club president. During his tenure the Council took over the ground and improved and extended the playing area. The Council also offered a co-tenancy to Walton Hockey Club, who were already renting a part of the land for their pitches, and in 1962 built a new pavilion for both clubs.

In 1968 the cricket club reached an arrangement with Rydens School under which a Colts team was established. The outstanding player to emerge was Monte Lynch, who came to Walton fron Guyana in 1971 (aged 13) and rapidly became a key member of the club XI. In 1977 he made his debut for Surrey; the following season he scored his maiden century for them, and soon established himself in the county side. Though originally selected as much for his spin bowling as his batting, he made his name as a big hitter, especially in limited-over matches. In 1981 he won an award for the greatest number of sixes (16) hit in a season in the John Player Sunday League.

Back in 1930 Walton Council had helped the cricket club to repossess its ground in Ashley Park; at the same time they supported the town's football team with a purchase of land for them in Stompond Lane. Once again George Froude was active in the matter, holding the chairmanship of Walton F.C. and arguing successfully against those who maintained that 'a good residential area' was no place for a stadium. Walton's first season there was 1933/4. Until then the team, which was founded at the turn of the century, had no permanent home ground, playing at different times at Elm Grove, Mount Felix, and locations in Annett Road, Terrace Road and Cottimore Lane. Even so, they achieved some success, entering the Amateur Cup for the first

**149** George Froude (1890-1959) was chairman of Walton Urban District Council in 1930/1 and of Walton and Weybridge Council in 1935/6 (when he presided at the opening of New Zealand Avenue) and again in 1941/2 and 1952/3. His service was recognised nationally by the award of an M.B.E. and locally by the naming after him of the recreation ground which lies between Sidney Road and Cottimore Lane.

time in 1907/8—and winning a first-round victory over Wimbledon—and becoming established in the Surrey Senior League. (The first game in that league, in 1922, was less happy, as the Walton and Aldershot teams went to each other's grounds! The game eventually kicked off in Walton, and Aldershot won 3-2.) Once at Stompond Lane the Walton team had several good seasons, heading the league in 1936/7. The Council co-operated by building a grandstand, formally opened in 1938 with a friendly against Fulham. But proposals for a merger with neighbouring Hersham F.C. were not pursued for the time being. Both teams were in the same league, and fans appreciated the local derbies between them.

**150**   Monte Lynch in 1995, after his retirement from county cricket, batting for Walton in an away match at Weybridge. The Weybridge wicket-keeper is L. Pettifer.

**151**   In 1907 Joseph Sassoon invited Walton Council to buy some land in Stompond Lane for use as a sports ground, but his offer was rejected. In 1933 the Council acquired the same piece of land as a permanent home for Walton F.C. A covered stand was opened in December 1938.

**152** The tennis club's airdome at Stompond Lane, which overcame some fierce local opposition and opened in 1973.

**153** Corinthian League champions, 1949.

The Council's development of Stompond Lane included the laying out of four tennis courts, and a Lawn Tennis Club was formed in 1939. Though its first full season was cut short by the outbreak of war, the club decided to keep going during hostilities, so as to offer recreation to London workers who had moved out to Walton. A membership of about 100 was maintained. This doubled after the war, and by 1952 there were seven courts available. Walton teams and players, notably the doubles pairing of John Archer and Jo Braithwaite, became very successful in county events. As the club flourished the possibility of an airdome for all-weather tennis began to be considered. At first this encountered much the same local hostility as the original proposal

for a Stompond Lane sports ground had done. One critic said it would be 'a ghastly sight which will disfigure the area'. However, in 1972 the council voted for the project to proceed. The dome was formally opened the next year, and the following season Walton was adjudged tennis's 'Club of the Year'. In recognition of this, one of the British finals for the Princess Sophia Cup, an international tournament for girls under 18, was played at Stompond Lane.

The football club also enjoyed success in the immediate post-war years. A merged Walton and Hersham F.C. was formed in 1945 and entered the Corinthian League, winning it in three successive seasons from 1946/7. They also reached the semi-finals of the

**154**   Amateur Cup winners, 1973.

Amateur Cup in 1951/2 and 1952/3: in March 1952 their quarter-final victory against Crook Town brought a record 10,000 crowd to Stompond Lane. However, these successes were followed by some lean years. Even though qualification for the F.A. Cup in 1957/8 meant a home tie against League opponents (3rd. Division Southampton) the outcome was a 6-1 defeat. The appointment of Allan Batsford as manager in 1967 brought a change of fortune. Walton and Hersham's next two cup encounters with League teams ended in victory. In 1972 Exeter City went down 2-1 at Stompond Lane. The following season Brighton and Hove Albion, then managed by Brian Clough, were held there to a no-score draw, and Walton and Hersham travelled to the south coast for a 4-0 win in the replay.

The club's crowning success came in the Amateur Cup, which they won in 1972/3 without conceding a goal. The first two rounds were played away from home. For the third round (against St Albans) a large crowd at Stompond Lane saw a game which was goalless at half-time, but Walton and Hersham scored five in the second half. The quarter-final and semi-final both finished goalless and had to be settled in replays. In the end, the local team met Slough Town in the final. It took place at Wembley on 14 April 1973. Attendance was 41,000: there is no record of how many came from Walton, but a good proportion of the town's population must have travelled to support the team. The only goal came in the 89th minute: Roger Connell scored it for Walton and Hersham, and football's Amateur Cup came to Stompond Lane.

## Postscript

Victory at Wembley was a high point for Walton. It put the town (briefly) on the sporting map and presaged the Football League management careers of Allan Batsford and the team's captain, Dave Bassett. But it also marked the ending of an era. The Amateur Cup, which Walton and Hersham defended unsuccessfully in 1973/4, was discontinued at the end of that season. It was one of the institutions which helped shape Walton's past but had no place in a modern world. Another was the Urban District, incorporated in Queen Victoria's reign but superseded by a larger authority in 1974. Other signs of modernity were the extinction of steam trains (the last scheduled service ran through Walton in 1967) and a decimal currency in place of '20 shillings in the pound'.

Old landmarks continued to vanish in the 1980s and '90s. Mayfield school made way for housing and the *Ashley Arms* for an office block. The Dental Factory closed its doors. British Rail and London Transport were privatised, so that Walton's public transport arrived in new colours from new companies. Even the town's recent buildings came under threat, with the town hall lost and the Centre, swimming pool and leisure centre all the subject of redevelopment plans. On the positive side, an up-to-date hospital and health centre took the place of the buildings which Dr Drabble had created, and the old barn at River House emerged as a brand-new centre for local arts.

Present-day Walton is thus a place of projects and blueprints, with much of its future still on the drawing board. But the town remains a good place to live—a close-knit community in a pleasant location by the Thames, well-rooted in its long and eventful past.

# Further Reading

**Publications of the Walton and Weybridge Local History Society**

Blackman, M.E., *Ashley Park* (1976); *A Short History of Walton-on-Thames* (1989)

Le Fevre, M., *300 years of local schools* (1970)

Martin, A.G., *Inns and Taverns in Walton and Weybridge* (1974, revised 1999)

Pulford, J.S.L. (ed.), *Memories of Old Walton and Weybridge* (1976); *Ashley Road School* (2000)

Stonebanks, J.A., *Mount Felix* (1978); *The Thames at Walton and Weybridge* (1980); *Cottimore and Walton Lodge* (1982)

**Other sources**

Barker, J.L. and D.M., *A window on Walton-on-Thames* (1994)

Dane, M., *The Sassoons of Ashley Park* (1999)

Greenwood, G.B., *Seventy-eight years of local government* (1974); *The charities of Walton-on-Thames* (1979); *Walton-on-Thames and Weybridge: a dictionary of local history* (1983)

Miller, K., *The History: Walton & Hersham Football Club* (1996)

Pevsner, N. and Nairn, I., *Buildings of England: Surrey* (Penguin, 1971)

Sandells, I.R., *The Church of Saint Mary Walton-on-Thames* (1992)

Skinner, L.F., *Methodism in Walton-on-Thames* (1979)

White, N., *Walton-on-Thames and Weybridge in Old Photographs* (1997)

**Material on Walton Studios**

Heppenstall, M., 'Walton's Little Hollywood—The Hepworth Studios'; 'Walton's Little Hollywood—The Nettlefold Studios'; *Journal of the Sunbury & Shepperton Local History Society* (1990)

Hepworth, C.M., *Came the Dawn* (Phoenix, 1951)

Warren, P., *British Film Studios: An Illustrated History* (Batsford, 1995)

# Index

References in **Bold** are to illustrations or captions on the page concerned

Walton in the 1960s (drawn by
J.C. Pulford).

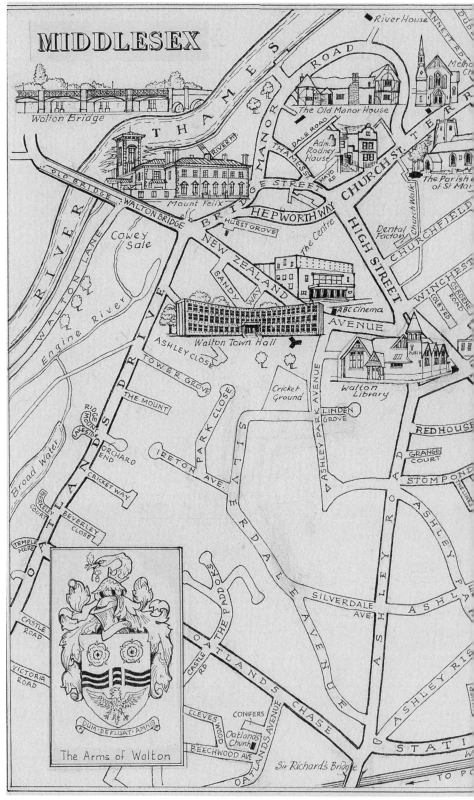